Kaneko's Story

Kaneko's Story

A CONVERSATION WITH KANEKO IKEDA

World Tribune
—*Press*—

Photos courtesy of Seikyo Press
Citations referring to *The Writings of Nichiren Daishonin*, volumes
I and II, are abbreviated as follows:

WND-(1 or 2), (page number)

Where appropriate, the titles of other books and magazines available
only in Japanese have been translated into English. They include:
A Teacher Named Takezawa (*Takezawa sensei to iu hito*; book)
Housewife's Companion (*Shufu no tomo*; magazine)
On Women (*Fujin-sho*; book)
That Road, This Road (*Ano michi, kono michi*; book)
The Tale of the Heike (*Heike monogatari*; book)
Women and Living (*Fujin to kurashi*; magazine)

Published by World Tribune Press
606 Wilshire Blvd.
Santa Monica, CA 90401

© 2008 Soka Gakkai

ISBN 978-1-932911-48-0 (hardcover)
ISBN 978-1-932911-51-0 (softcover)

Interior and cover designed by Gopa & Ted2, Inc.

10 9 8 7 6 5 4 3 2 1

Contents

Foreword

I LOVE MY MOTHER and the way she lives: sincerely, honestly, embracing her mission in life with integrity. I see her as an ordinary woman who exemplifies greatness.

I do not remember her ever raising her voice even once to me or my brothers. Her perennial smile, no matter what the situation, is what I remember. I see her as a woman no hardship can defeat.

She stands firm in the face of every storm; she forges ahead with strength and courage. How profound the convictions that must lie behind her smile; how powerful the hope she must hold in her heart. What I can say is what many friends around the world have said about her: Her wonderful smile deeply encourages me.

The first edition of this book was published in 2005. More than ten years before that, we were warmly invited by *Housewife's Companion*, a leading women's magazine in Japan, to publish a book with my mother's smile as its theme. Though flattered, my mother firmly declined their offer. This was natural for a woman who prefers to avoid the limelight.

The relationship my parents and the Soka Gakkai have with *Housewife's Companion*, however, is deep, extending over many years. In the summer of 1957, the magazine published an article profiling my parents' mentor, second Soka Gakkai president Josei Toda, and his wife. Then, in the autumn of 1963, three years after my father was inaugurated president of the Soka Gakkai, the magazine ran his first interview. Since then, *Housewife's Companion* has published New Year's messages from my father, as well as his dialogue with the writer Sawako Ariyoshi. They also interviewed my parents together. In these and other ways, the humanitarian message of the SGI has been communicated to the magazine's many women readers.

The magazine's parent company, Shufu No Tomo Publishers, also published my father's bestselling book *On Women*, as well as the Japanese-language edition of his dialogue with American futurist Hazel Henderson titled *Planetary Citizenship*.

Eventually my mother felt we should show our appreciation by accepting their subsequent invitation to publish *Kaneko's Story*.

Some of the topics explored are her childhood memories, her friendships, her relationship with her mentor, youth and marriage, supporting a husband who bears a global responsibility, the wisdom of a homemaker and mother, her courage in surmounting life's trials, dialogues with friends around the world, and her philosophy of peace, happiness, and health.

The conversation in this book highlights, in a warm and delightful way, the power of my mother's smile and draws from her stories that even my family had not heard before. The *Kaneko* of the title is the name my parents' mentor, Josei Toda, chose to call her as a sign of affection. He was ahead of his time then, as always, in that the Chinese character for the middle syllable, *ne*, was only recently given a place on the list of characters eligible for use in personal names. When my mother was younger, that same Mr. Toda gave her a copy of the *Gosho Zenshu* (The Collected Writings of Nichiren Daishonin) with the following *waka* poem penned by him on the front page:

> *May your gentle image in the moonlight*
> *be filled with the strength of the Mystic Law.*

Just as Mr. Toda's poem intimates, my mother lives a life as fresh and exhilarating as moonlight. I am sure her attitude toward life will never change.

Nothing would give our family more joy than if this book conveys to readers the bright glow of my mother's gentle but strong spirit as inspiration for a century in which women shall shine.

—Hiromasa Ikeda, eldest son of Kaneko Ikeda
Autumn 2004

Introduction

AN ENCOUNTER WITH DESTINY—haven't we all experienced it at least once? Perhaps it was with a sweetheart, a spouse, teacher, or friend. How often do these fateful encounters bring happiness?

The story on these pages is about a young girl named Kane Shiraki who awaited her own such encounter. She met her destiny when she met Daisaku Ikeda, who later became the third president of the Soka Gakkai. Kane Shiraki married him, changing her name to Kaneko Ikeda. The interview for this book began with her statement that meeting Mr. Ikeda has been the source of her lifelong happiness. These pages provide a glimpse into the surprising power of this reserved woman, which is perhaps the force that draws happiness to her.

Underlying her magnetic persona is the power of love. It might also be called the power of effort, wisdom, and character. Each of us has something in our own heart that enables us to find these qualities in another.

Important things most often exist unassumingly amid the

ordinary. In Kaneko Ikeda's quiet, cheerful expression, in her pleasant smile that gives happiness to those around her, we may find a secret we all seek, the secret to attracting good fortune.

Mrs. Ikeda was born on February 27, 1932, the third of four children, to Shigeji and Shizuko Shiraki. Firstborn was her sister, Yoshi. Next came Fumio, her older brother, then Kane, and finally her younger brother, Shuji. The Shiraki family lived in Yaguchi-no-Watashi in Ota Ward, Tokyo. Mrs. Ikeda's early life is typical of Japanese families in the Showa period, the years in Japanese history spanning 1926 to 1989, which saw war, poverty, and reconstruction.

The conversation on the following pages zeroes in on her talent for drawing happiness to herself and those close to her, including her husband, Daisaku Ikeda, as told in their own words.

1

A Young Girl Awaits Her Destiny

In what kind of family did you grow up, and what lessons learned from your parents do you cherish even now?

I had a very peaceful and harmonious family life. From my perspective and that of my siblings, my parents had a close relationship.

My husband often remarks that a harmonious family life is a precious and indispensable experience for the children as well as for the husband and wife.

My father was an ordinary man. He had a serious disposition and was committed to his family, so we had a tranquil home life. I remember that when I was a child, my father would ring the bell at the front gate upon his return home from work, and then the entire family would line up at the entryway to welcome him home.

Probably because I grew up with this custom, after I married, I greeted my husband in the same way when he returned home. When my husband and I lived in

Kobayashi-cho in Ota Ward (currently East Yaguchi), the children were too young to observe this routine. Then, in 1966, we moved to Shinano-machi in Shinjuku. Our eldest son, Hiromasa, was in his first year of junior high school; our second son, Shirohisa, was in sixth grade; and our third son, Takahiro, was in second grade. When my husband returned home and the boys were still awake, though our house was rather small, I would use the intercom that could be heard in each room to let the boys know that their father was home. They would come out to greet him, then go back to their rooms. This is how I was brought up, and after I married, this custom became a natural part of my new family's daily life.

My father was conscientious, so he was at times a strict disciplinarian. I don't recall, however, that he ever used force to discipline us children. The way in which we greeted people was one area in which my parents were very particular. When we returned home, we announced our return to our parents. I believe that it is important to teach children proper greetings. If children can greet people properly, then they are on their way to developing good communication skills. Beginning a greeting with a comment about the season may be a unique Japanese custom. This habit of starting with something that both parties can share reveals a thoughtfulness that I think is beautiful and appealing. I hope that, no matter how the times change, this aspect of Japanese sensibility is never lost.

My mother was an avid student. She was proactive in pursuing her interests. She also liked anything new. They would call women like her "Miss High Collar," an English-language expression used in Japan at the time to mean "fashionable."

My mother's family came from Gifu Prefecture where, long ago, her family members were village leaders. My mother graduated from a girls' high school at a time when it was rare for a girl to receive a high school education. Perhaps because of that influence, she liked the atmosphere of the Free School, founded by Motoko Hani of Fujin No Tomo Publishers, and so she gathered people in her neighborhood for discussion groups and often visited Fujin No Tomo's offices. She seemed to be fascinated with the Taisho era (1912–1926) democratic movement and the humanitarianism of writers such as Saneatsu Mushanokouji and Takeo Arishima.

My mother made it a habit always to stay busy. Even when she was ill, she would get up as soon as she started feeling better and busy herself as usual. This is a lasting impression. My mother did not have a strong constitution, so my sister and I often helped with the housework.

My mother was the kind of person who treated everything with care. She was adamant about never wasting food. We naturally learned these values as we were growing up. My mother impressed upon us the importance of these traditional values while teaching us to be practical.

My father, with his robust and frank personality, disliked dealing with minutiae. No doubt this is why he sought out a woman like my mother.

I was the third of four children. My sister was the

oldest, and I had a brother three years my elder and a younger brother. It was a tradition in the Shiraki family to give female children simple, two-syllable names written in *kana* (a Japanese system of phonetic writing). My older sister was named *Yoshi*, and I was given the name *Kane* by our grandfather.

When I married, my mentor, Josei Toda, gave me a new name—*Kaneko*—and wrote it in Chinese characters in what was then the modern style. I have been using the name he gave me ever since. My parents were happy with my new name and remarked that they wished they had named me that from the start. I have not, however, changed my legal name, which remains *Kane*.

My brothers and sister and I were brought up during the war and postwar period, so I believe my parents endured great hardship raising our family. My father worked for a sugar company, but because of the war, the company could not continue to do business. Besides that, we had to evacuate Tokyo. We sought refuge in my parents' hometown, deep in the mountains of Gifu Prefecture. At that time, all four of us were still young, and I sensed that my parents were going through the most difficult period of their lives. Of course, dealing with the tragedies caused by war was the reality confronting families all over Japan.

Nothing inflicts more misfortune and misery on ordinary people than war. We must never permit such horrors to be visited on humankind again. I really admire people of my parents' generation who, even while enduring the injustice and indignities of war, continued to live and care for their families without losing hope.

Having become a parent myself, I know it is difficult to raise children even in times of peace, so I cannot imagine the hardships that my parents must have experienced. I have discussed this issue with my husband, and we agree that, no matter what hardships one may have raising children, the lessons of raising them through those hardships become priceless treasures.

What led to your encounter with the Soka Gakkai? Were there any changes in your family after you became members?

My mother decided that we were to become Soka Gakkai members. After I was born, she had a difficult recovery. She contracted thrombophlebitis, in which blood clots form in the veins. Unless the person stays at rest, the blood clots may enter the lungs, which could be fatal. Nowadays, there is medicine to manage the condition, but in those days medicine was difficult to obtain.

My mother's legs were always swollen. I think this was why I never clung to my mother, expecting her to baby me. My younger brother—who was the baby—needed her attention more than I did. Perhaps this is why I learned to endure adversity and developed patience.

Our next-door neighbor, who was concerned about my mother's health, encouraged us to become members of the Soka Gakkai. After about a year of indecision, my mother joined. My father opposed her decision at first, but once my mother had made up her mind, it naturally followed that my father also joined.

Our entire family became members on July 12, 1941. I was in the fourth grade at Yaguchi Elementary School. Because the difficulties accompanying my birth were the reason my mother joined the Soka Gakkai, my mother told my elder sister, "That child has a deep connection to Buddhism."

When I was in the fifth grade, my homeroom teacher was Mr. Takehisa Tsuji. He was a disciple of the second Soka Gakkai president, Josei Toda, and a longtime leader in the Soka Gakkai organization. He now serves on the executive advisory council. So I guess my mother was right about my connection to Buddhism.

In those days, we held Soka Gakkai discussion meetings at our home and, on occasion, founding president Tsunesaburo Makiguchi attended. My mother would go to the train station to meet him. The surrounding area had few houses and only a few shops in front of the station. It was so sparsely developed that we could see the banks of the Tama River from there.

My mother would meet Mr. Makiguchi with me in tow, and he would pat me on the head and say: "Thank you! Thank you for coming."

Mr. Makiguchi seemed quite old to me, but when he spoke at our group meetings, his dignified presence was accentuated by his perfectly upright posture and sonorous voice. This was during the war, and I recall one occasion when three members of the Special Higher Police (also known as the "thought police") came and sat in the hallway to observe the meeting. While Mr. Makiguchi was talking, they would often interrupt, yelling out: "Stop there! Disband the meeting!"

Even in my childhood innocence, I was worried about this. My mother calmed me by saying: "Mr. Makiguchi is right. He is brave and firm in his beliefs, so there is nothing to be afraid of."

I am grateful to my parents that we were blessed with a wonderful home life. My father was an ordinary man, but one who was amazingly broad-minded and tolerant. My mother, on the other hand, was straightforward in declaring her opinions. After she became a Soka Gakkai member, she was strict regarding matters of faith. I appreciate the respective roles that my mother and father played in our family.

My father lived to a robust eighty-five years. My mother, who recovered completely from her illness, involved herself in Soka Gakkai activities and traveled around the entire country. She continued energetically to provide encouragement to others until she died at ninety-five.

Did you get along well with your siblings when you were growing up?

I was the third of four children, and so in the Shiraki household, I was low on the totem pole. My older brother and sister had high expectations placed upon them and were treated accordingly, reflecting my parents' own upbringing in the countryside where feudalistic thinking still flourished. Looking back, however, I feel that this situation was very fortunate for me. I mean, according to Japanese tradition, I was not expected to be responsible for maintaining family ties. My husband's position in the Soka Gakkai organization entails so many obligations that it is not possible for me to interact with my relatives as much as I would like.

My husband was the fifth son, and so he grew up relatively free from traditional Japanese demands to be his family's caregiver. While I have not neglected my Shiraki relatives, my position as the younger daughter has let me off the hook to some degree.

When I have to choose between a Soka Gakkai event and a family activity, the former takes precedence.

My older brother was competitive and my older sister had a mind of her own, so they often got into sibling spats. I respected my older sister very much. She excelled in her studies and was never reluctant to speak her mind. I couldn't hold a candle to her. My older brother and I were three years apart, but we got along fine.

Looking at your school records, I see you were class president for a trimester each in the second and third grades, vice president in the fourth grade, and class president again for a trimester each in the fifth and sixth grades. After elementary school, you went on to a girls' high school.

Both my older sister and I attended Chofu Academy (currently, Den'en Chofu Academy), a private girls' school. Its motto is "Devotion." The school placed great emphasis on student responsibilities such as cleaning the classrooms, the auditorium and the restrooms.

Before I enrolled in the school, my father went to take a look and immediately liked what he saw. On the school campus was a bronze statue of the founder, Shohei Nishimura, standing proudly with mop in hand and a bucket by his side.

The school traditions must have matched perfectly with my father's philosophy. He was obstinate when it came to certain things. My older sister was the first to enter the school, and it was understood that I would also attend when I was old enough. There were other good public girls' schools near our house that many of my friends attended, but my parents did not consider having me take the entrance exam for any school but Chofu Academy. If they had been like other parents, I would have been instructed to take the exams for public schools along with my friends.

My husband's father also insisted on getting his way if he was convinced that he was right, to the extent that he was nicknamed "Mr. Stubborn." He had an antiwar philosophy, and in this respect, he had much in common with my father. This became even clearer after I married into the Ikeda family.

Do you have many photographs from your childhood days?

Not many photos from my childhood remain. Most of them were destroyed by fire in the air raids during the war. On April 13, 1945, my mother, my two brothers, and I evacuated to Gifu Prefecture. There was a system in place for the group evacuation of elementary-school children, but feeling it would be too sad for my younger brother to have to go without us, we all went together to my parents' hometown.

On the train to Gifu, we heard that the American president, Franklin D. Roosevelt, had died (April 12, 1945). We all speculated that, because of his death, the war would be over soon. We thought we could all turn around and go back home.

As we soon discovered, nothing could have been further from the truth. Two days later, we learned that the area where we lived in Tokyo had been bombed in what became known as the Great Tokyo Air Raid. It followed an air raid in March, and lasted from April 13 to 15, 1945. Omori and Kamata were hit on April 15.

My father and older sister had stayed behind to make arrangements to send our belongings before following us to Gifu. The air raid struck before they could finish. They had to take with them what they could and flee for their lives.

In those days, my father enjoyed a good drink, so he dug a hole in a field, buried some sake in it, and covered it with tatami mats. Among the burned-out ruins of our home, all that survived was his stash of sake.

In that area, only two houses remained unscathed, and they belonged to Soka Gakkai members. My father was fond of saying that he later visited those members and celebrated their good fortune with his sake.

After arriving in Gifu, we had no way of knowing the extent of the fire damage in Tokyo. Television was unheard of by most people, and almost no one had telephones.

Until that point, I had been attending a private girls' school and could not transfer to a prefectural school, so it was decided that I would attend a municipal school. School registration was the reason my older brother and I came to stay with our maternal aunt, who lived in Misono- cho in Gifu City, and my mother and younger brother stayed in my mother's family home in Fukutomi, outside the city. And so we began our lives as wartime evacuees, separated from one another by the Nagara River.

After a while, we received a postcard from my father informing us of the fire damage in Tokyo. Then, on the night of July 9, 1945, just one month before the end of the war, Gifu City was also subjected to air raids. (B-29 bombers unloaded their deadly cargo, and approximately 70 percent of the city center was destroyed by fire.) My older brother was only in junior high school then, but men were needed to fight the fires, so he and my uncle were called on to join the fire brigade. The rest of us—my aunt, her two children, and I—escaped with our lives.

Turning to look behind us, we could see the firebombs raining down on the city, and I could not help but be amazed at how accurately they were falling on the city center.

We passed victims along the road and could hardly bear to see their pitifully charred and unrecognizable bodies. We crossed the great Nagara River Bridge, joining the masses of refugees streaming out of the city. Along the way, we stopped to rest in a mulberry grove whose trees were bare. It comforted me to think of ourselves as additions to their branches.

"They say 'mulberry grove, mulberry grove' to ward off lightning strikes," I suddenly blurted. Everyone burst out laughing. It seemed like such a weird thing to say when our situation was so dire.

When morning came, we started back toward the city, and as far as we could see, almost everything was burned to ruins. Our place was burned to the ground, but the house of someone my aunt knew, perhaps a relative, was still standing, and we assembled there. We were very concerned about my uncle and brother and wanted to go look for them, but they arrived safely soon after. I suppose that was natural; there was no place else to go. Mysteriously, my father, who must have been worried about us, showed up also, so we were all reunited.

Your younger brother has commented, "Our mother often said about Kane, 'She never gets angry, no matter what is

*said to her.' I thought it was surprising that even though
evacuee children were often bullied and ridiculed by the
local children, they never bothered Kane."*

(Mrs. Ikeda laughs at the thought.) That's not true. I did
get bullied. I did have difficult times. I got angry when
the situation warranted it, and I also had some bitter
experiences.

What books impressed you as a young girl?

I'd have to say the books of Nobuko Yoshiya. I still
remember her book *That Road, This Road*, about two
girls born on the same day who are switched at birth.
One grows up in an affluent household and the other in a
poor family. The outcome of the story is similar to that of
The Prince and the Pauper. This story is still close to my
heart. Then there is Yuzo Yamamoto's work *The Rock
by the Roadside*, which I read with tears streaming down
my cheeks. I also enjoyed the Western works *Wuthering
Heights* and *Gone With the Wind*.

Did you return to Tokyo immediately after the war ended?

On August 15, 1945, we welcomed the end of the war,
still living where we had taken refuge. The sugar business
where my father worked depended on overseas trade, and

because Japan had just lost the war, it would be a long time before he could work there again. My father also seemed to feel that it would be better to settle down in Gifu. I was in my second year of junior high school and very much wanted to return to Tokyo. This was the only time I can remember being so insistent and uncompromising.

The war ended during the last part of my first semester that year. I spent my second semester in Gifu, and then I was allowed to go with my older brother to live with my aunt on my father's side in Kikuna, Yokohama. This was so I could commute to my old school, Den'en Chofu Academy. We were to stay with my aunt until our family could build a temporary shelter at our previous residence.

At that time, my uncle had passed away and my two cousins had not yet returned from the battlefront. Since my aunt was living alone, she kindly invited us to stay with her. She was my father's older sister and quite elderly, so I fondly called her "Grandma" rather than "Auntie." I wanted to make myself useful to her, so I helped in the kitchen and in cleaning the house.

One morning, as I was opening the rain shutters, I found myself face to face with the next-door neighbor. We exchanged greetings, and he said, "I haven't seen such a real human face in a long time." I was still basically a child, and so I laughingly responded, "What does that mean?"

His words left a lasting impression on me, though. Now that I think of it, at that time I had already joined the Soka Gakkai and had been diligent in the daily practice of chanting Nam-myoho-renge-kyo. In the inhumane and confusing times of the immediate postwar period, the face of a young girl with such strong Buddhist faith must have seemed somehow peaceful and serene.

After returning to Yaguchi-no-Watashi from Kikuna, I continued attending school and took a part-time job on weekends in hopes of contributing to the family finances. I would take the train to the bread factory in Shinagawa, where I worked on Saturdays and Sundays. I may have gotten the job through my father's contacts in the sugar business.

In those days, the factory only produced loaves of bread for school lunches. Later on, the factory began to manufacture bread rolls. I had not known how to make bread before taking this job, so I was fascinated. I was always completely amazed when the bakers would take leftover dough and show off their skills by making swirled rolls, crab shapes and other creations.

I also held a part-time job at the nearby hospital for about a year and a half. It was within walking distance of our house. I was invited to help out perhaps because I had been there when my mother was an outpatient. I helped sterilize syringes, wrap powdered medicine, and check insurance.

While in elementary school, I took an extra-curricular calligraphy class, although I had to drop it when the teacher became ill. Later, when I worked at a bank, I learned stenography. Both these skills proved to be very useful, even now.

*It seems that your experience at Chofu Academy was
a precious one.*

I am very happy that I was blessed with good friends
and teachers. My lifelong friendships with classmates are
priceless treasures that I would not trade for anything in
the world. I had so many wonderful teachers, including
my homeroom teacher, Miss Tomiko Maeda, and the
chairman of the board, Mr. Masanaru Shimada, who
taught social studies. Even after I graduated, these teachers kindly looked out for me in many ways. I have come
to feel immensely grateful for such wonderful teachers.

*Now I would like to share some thoughts of people from
your alma mater, including the late Mr. Shimada, and some
of your classmates, including Ms. Taeko Kaga:*

I have had the opportunity to counsel more than eight
thousand students, but I must say that Kaneko stood out
head and shoulders above the rest. Even now, I clearly
remember that when we would meet in the halls, she
would stop and greet me with a deep bow, her school-
girl braids dangling. Every year, when I receive her New
Year's card wishing me well, it is heartwarming.

Masanaru Shimada
Former Chairman of the Board, Chofu Academy

From the very beginning, our homeroom teacher, Ms. Tomiko Maeda, noticed Kaneko. When Kaneko came to visit the school with her older sister, it was Ms. Maeda who met with them. She liked the way Kaneko straightened her shoes neatly at the entryway and bowed with lovely manners. Ms. Maeda even went so far as to personally confirm that Kaneko had passed the entrance examination. She remarked, "That is the kind of young lady we want to enroll in our school."

⬛ ⬛ ⬛

After enrolling, Kaneko became the class monitor. Students were chosen to be class monitors because they were good students and also because they were well-mannered and refined. Kaneko did such a good job that the teachers often said among themselves, "We have complete confidence that the class is being managed well," and "That class is a model class."

⬛ ⬛ ⬛

Kaneko would take the lead in wiping down the hallways. We classmates all agreed that she best embodied the values and spirit of Chofu Academy.

⬛ ⬛ ⬛

Ms. Maeda would often say, "Kaneko is so sweet, yet she has the courage to speak out clearly against injustice."

⬛ ⬛ ⬛

When Ms. Maeda heard about Kaneko's marriage to Daisaku Ikeda, she was delighted. She said: "I am so happy for them. They are a fine couple, and I am sure that they will build a wonderful Soka Gakkai organization." Ms. Maeda attended Soka Gakkai events and also visited the community center in Ota Ward and Soka University in Hachioji. After each visit, she would talk about her experiences in the teachers' lounge, and the teachers as well as the principal were all impressed.

■ ■ ■

In the summer of 2002, Ms. Maeda passed away at the age of ninety-six. Kaneko, who was attending an event far away, could not attend the funeral. She sent a moving telegram of condolence that included the following poem:

"The light of the firefly, snow on the windowsill.
"Our teacher has lovingly watched over us for so
many years.

"I will never forget the great debt I owe to Tomiko Maeda, my beloved, kind, and superbly intelligent teacher. I will hold her memory in my heart as I live in the manner she would expect of her students.

"Thank you, Ms. Maeda, for all you mean to us. Please rest in peace.

"Goodbye, dear Ms. Maeda."

Ms. Maeda's family was deeply moved by Kaneko's words.

Kaneko is a very kind-hearted person who is always concerned about the welfare of others. She is a wonderful
person who treats others with fairness and dignity. At
class reunions, whenever I have occasion to meet her, I
am happy to discover that she has not changed a bit.

*Please tell us about where your path took you after gradu-
ation. What led you to take a job at a bank? What did you
learn from your job?*

After graduation, I applied for several jobs and was hired
in 1950. Unlike today, there was no concept of career
advancement for women. Only five years had passed
since the war ended, and the restoration of Tokyo was
still a long way off. In those days, a job in a bank was
very steady and desirable work for a woman. Other jobs
suitable for women at the time, such as being a nurse or
a schoolteacher, required additional training. I think my
father also felt that a bank job was reliable and steady
work.

Today, from the time they start school until graduation, students have a much broader range of occupations
to consider and more freedom in doing so. I wonder if
I would have followed the same path—entering a girls'
school and working in a bank—if I had come of age in
today's world.

Actually, as graduation approached, I wavered about

whether to pursue further education. My father sent my sister and me to a girls' school for practical reasons, believing that scholarship was not necessary for girls. Although my sister went on to study nutrition, my father advised me that, since I had completed high school under the new postwar system, I should get a job.

At that time, there were not many schools beyond high school. Even so, some of my classmates were taking entrance exams for institutions of higher learning. This made my heart waver. When I was a senior, I worked part-time at a hospital and entertained the idea of becoming a physician. The company where my father had worked had not yet recovered from the war, and the cost of attending medical school was quite high. I considered other options such as studying pharmacology.

My parents told me to decide for myself, so I earnestly chanted Nam-myoho-renge-kyo. Finally, I decided to apply for a job. This was the first time that I truly felt that I had come to a decision on my own. Until that point, my faith had been based on following what my parents and family were doing. In the morning, I was not allowed to eat breakfast if I hadn't done my morning sutra recitation. This was the first time I prayed earnestly and felt decisive about a choice I had made. I felt completely certain and determined. After I made up my mind, I began to see all the advantages of getting a job. Also, because my older sister had just gotten married and I knew the family's financial situation, I felt that it was important for me to help out even a little with the family finances.

Now that I had decided to get a job, I began to pray to work for a bank. I was immediately hired upon being interviewed. The bank was Sumitomo. I chose Sumitomo simply because their recruiter was one of the first to come to our school. I interviewed with them and later with a recruiter from another bank. Both offered me a position, but I received Sumitomo's offer first. In addition, my school recommended that company.

If I had decided to pursue higher education, I might never have met my husband, Daisaku Ikeda. *(Her face lights up with a happy smile.)*

I believe that choosing to work was a fortuitous decision in my life.

When I started to work, it was difficult to buy clothes because they were still rationed. Of course, companies did not require uniforms back then. So, I sewed some outfits out of old clothes. That's how I learned to sew.

My first responsibilities were keeping track of receipts and disbursements. I was learning on the job, but I was in charge of totaling the entire day's transactions. That required an abacus, and because I hadn't used one since my school days, I practiced at home. When I started working at the bank, I asked if it was all right that I was not very good at using an abacus and was told it wouldn't be a problem. Eventually, I became pretty good at it.

I worked at the bank for only two years, and toward the end of that period I won first prize in an abacus contest held at our branch. Even after calculators became popular, I still used the abacus.

If I did not finish totaling all the day's transactions during work hours, I had to work overtime. If the balance was off by even one yen, I had to redo the entire calculation. This attitude—that today's work must be finished today—has stood me in good stead in my marriage as well.

Even now, I feel that finishing today's tasks today is a valuable habit that has been a great advantage, especially in managing household accounts. When I got married, Mr. Toda emphasized to me the importance of keeping household accounts. It was as if my work at the bank was a rehearsal for married life. That, too, was my good fortune.

My mother was also diligent about keeping the household books. I have heard that in other countries, such as Germany, home economics principles are taken seriously in the maintenance of the household. I read somewhere that this tradition, kept by German housewives, formed part of the basis on which the nation's public finance system was developed. My mother seemed to value such sound practices. Perhaps she kept household accounts because it suited her personality, but I also think it was because she studied household management.

After getting married, thanks to having worked in one, I felt very comfortable using a bank. (*Mrs. Ikeda laughs at the memory of her earliest experiences with banks.*)

Every payday, I would deposit my entire pay at our local bank. Going to the bank was such a chore that I would try as much as possible to make due with whatever cash I had on hand, and when I did withdraw money, it was only a small amount. Before I worked at the bank, my perception was that it would be embarrassing to deposit or withdraw anything but large sums of money. On the contrary, however, working there I learned that banks welcomed small transactions. I withdrew relatively small amounts such as one thousand or three thousand yen with no embarrassment whatsoever.

There were many other reasons why I felt that working at the bank was good for me. I learned a lot about relating to other people. I had attended a girls' school, and so at my workplace, for the first time, I found myself in an environment with men. It was a socialization experience and an opportunity to learn how to interact with people.

Did you worry about how to manage both your work and your Soka Gakkai activities?

In 1950, the same year I began working, it was increasingly clear that Mr. Toda would be inaugurated as the second president of the Soka Gakkai. On May 3 of the following year, the long-awaited ceremony to appoint him second president was held. That summer, on July 19, the young women's division was formed, and I participated as one of the first seventy-four young women.

The plan was to have everyone sing together after the inaugural ceremony. Suddenly, out of the blue, someone appointed me to be the lead singer. I didn't know what to do, but Mr. Toda covered for me. He said, "A leader must make sure that a colleague likes singing in front of people before asking her to do so." Mr. Toda had come to my family's home for discussion meetings, so he knew me well and protected me at every opportunity.

My first year on the job, I had to immerse myself completely in my work. That is probably why I developed skill in using the abacus. During that period, I felt that I must at least attend Soka Gakkai discussion meetings. In the second year, my job responsibility changed from accounting to general affairs. Gradually, I became better at managing my time, so that I could attend Soka Gakkai functions and still devote myself to my work.

This is true today as well. I have found that making time for both Soka Gakkai activities and work or family responsibilities is easy to say but difficult to achieve. I am convinced, however, that the effort to balance both organizational and other responsibilities is important for one's future, because doing so expands one's state of life, brings good fortune and vitality and becomes the foundation for a broader, richer life experience.

2

Love and Marriage

THE YOUNG MAN who was to shape the destiny of nineteen-year-old Kane Shiraki was a complete contrast to her father, Shigeji. His name was Daisaku Ikeda, as skinny as a rail and with a constitution weakened by tuberculosis.

Josei Toda was a mentor to both Kane and Daisaku and is said to have lamented with tears in his eyes, "Daisaku may not live past the age of thirty." It was a dismal prediction, but Mr. Ikeda was an extraordinary youth who amazed everyone who knew him.

He was extraordinary but so physically weak that he was not expected to survive beyond thirty. The young man carried a considerable handicap. Kaneko, however, did not perceive him as handicapped. "I sensed in him a powerful and expansive presence. There was something remarkable and appealing about him," she says of her early impression. At the time of their first encounter, it seems she saw beneath the surface and into the man's true essence.

The young Ikeda was oblivious to the scrutiny of those around him and always seemed calm and composed. This perhaps played in his favor. He was the type that Kaneko liked to root for.

Kaneko Ikeda is a positive thinker. She evaluates every situation calmly and favors ideas that point in a positive direction. In her decisions to sew her own clothes or challenge her skills on the abacus, she took ownership of her experience and proceeded with confidence and responsibility. Describing this reserved and beautiful girl, her teacher Ms. Maeda commented, "She is so sweet, yet she has the courage to speak out forthrightly against injustice."

The July 1966 issue of *Housewife's Companion* recorded a meeting between the thirty-eight-year-old Soka Gakkai president, Daisaku Ikeda, and the award-winning author Sawako Ariyoshi. It was six years after Daisaku's inauguration as president. The following is an excerpt from that discussion:

Ikeda: My wife is a very quiet and shy person. She seldom says a word about my activities. We were married in 1952, the year after our mentor, Mr. Toda, became president of the Soka Gakkai. On May 3, 1960, I became Soka Gakkai president, and when I returned home that day, my wife told me, "I consider your inauguration ceremony a funeral service."

Ariyoshi: She called the ceremony a funeral? That doesn't sound like something a quiet and shy person would say.

Regarding this episode, which later became very well known, Mrs. Ikeda smiled and said, "I think I was responding to my husband's feeling [that his new responsibility would require his complete commitment in terms of time and energy]." Learning from his example, she was inspired to take full responsibility for the family so that her husband could devote himself wholeheartedly to the movement for peace. She had become the kind of wife who could face this reality.

Around the time that Kaneko was becoming aware of the young Daisaku as a romantic young man with big dreams and a trustworthy character, a major shift was occurring in Daisaku Ikeda's heart. The young and determined Daisaku was surely aware of Kaneko's qualities. Their marriage would have a major impact on the future of the Soka Gakkai.

Mr. Ikeda wrote in a memoir published by the *Nihon Keizai Shimbun* (Japan's leading financial newspaper):

> It was in the summer of 1951 that I suddenly became aware of the young woman who would become my wife. There was a boy named Shiraki among the junior high school students sent to work at the Niigata Ironworks in Kamata where I was working. I learned later that his family had joined the Soka Gakkai before the war. That summer, on the way home from a Soka Gakkai group meeting, he introduced his younger sister to me. She worked at a bank downtown. After that, we had occasion to see each other quite often.

What was your impression of your future husband when you met him on the way home from that meeting?

The meeting was one in a series of lectures given by Mr. Toda on the writings of Nichiren. It was held every Friday at the small Soka Gakkai Headquarters in Nishi-Kanda of Tokyo's Chiyoda Ward. It was so popular that, unless you arrived early, you could not even get into the room. The place was always so packed that people were crowded all the way to the stairs. My older brother and I always attended.

One day, my brother and Daisaku recognized each other and exchanged greetings. During the war, when he worked at the Niigata Ironworks, Daisaku had formed a reading group with his friends to exchange ideas. My older brother had attended the group. After the war, everyone went their separate ways, and the two did not meet again until that moment several years later.

After the Friday lecture, since Daisaku lived in Omori and he, my brother, and I were all going in that direction, we boarded the same train. I was standing beside my brother, hanging on to the passenger strap. My brother turned to Daisaku and introduced me, saying, "This is my sister."

Daisaku said something like, "Oh, hi!" and we exchanged nods. Then he and my brother continued talking. That was our first meeting.

After that, we had a number of opportunities to go home on the same train. Mr. Tsuji, my homeroom teacher from elementary school, also was going home in the same direction, so I would chat with Mr. Tsuji, and my brother would talk with my future husband. At that time, Daisaku and I did not pay much attention to each other.

We both belonged to the same Soka Gakkai chapter, Kamata Chapter. In 1952, to commemorate the seven-hundredth anniversary of the founding of Nichiren Buddhism, the Soka Gakkai published the *Gosho Zenshu* (The Collected Writings of Nichiren Daishonin). The members in our chapter discussed how many copies we would each purchase. Daisaku, who had helped with the editing, said he would take one hundred copies. At twelve hundred yen per copy, that was a considerable sum in those days.

Most of the others were ordering two or three, at the most five, copies. Then Daisaku came along and announced that he wanted one hundred copies!

He was like that. He stood out from everyone else. When my mother heard about it, since she and he were both leaders in the same Soka Gakkai group, she called him "a big *furoshiki*" (a cloth used to wrap and carry things), which is a cute way of calling him a big talker. I had a completely different reaction. He impressed me as a powerful and dynamic person. Those qualities attracted me to him.

What my mother and others actually meant was, "Mr. Ikeda goes overboard."

But as my husband once said, "Don't worry, I'll just use that big *furoshiki* to wrap everything up and deliver." I am the type to applaud a line like that.

Occasionally when we met, we would walk together along the banks of the Tama River and talk about everything from world affairs to the universe. Our discussions would range from the stars in the night sky to the state of the Soka Gakkai and its future plans. I listened, trying to take it all in, but it was all I could do just to keep up with the grand scale of his thoughts. Daisaku was attracted to the philosophy of Yukichi Fukuzawa, the founder of Keio University, and he often spoke of Fukuzawa's idea of "developing the mind of the people," explaining it in a way that even someone like me could understand. The concept "mind of the people" refers to the people's spiritual and emotional state and that, by developing this, a true civilization becomes possible for the first time. Daisaku described this idea as one of Fukuzawa's most important teachings.

After a discussion like this, Daisaku would recommend this or that book. He liked to discuss books with me. He enthusiastically recommended books such as Yoshiro Nagayo's *A Teacher Named Takezawa* and a collection of poems by Lord Byron, and so I read them. Another book he suggested was *Napoleon* by Yusuke Tsurumi.

Of all the books recommended by your husband, which one impressed you the most?

The Count of Monte Cristo by Alexandre Dumas and Victor Hugo's *Les Misérables* were most memorable to me. My husband was devoted to literature in his youth, and he strongly opposed social and institutional abuses. He often said that organizations should be humane. Mr. Toda also had this in mind when he told my husband, "Why don't you make the Soka Gakkai organization into one that is consistent with your ideals?" Daisaku would tell me that he wanted to build an organization in which everyone could wholeheartedly and joyfully participate. Our discussions were often about such ideals.

Mr. Toda declared at our wedding that "men must have strength." I think that women are attracted to men who are both strong and uphold high ideals. At that time, there were not many romantics like him who were filled with big dreams. It is said that young women often compare men with their fathers.

In his address at our wedding, Mr. Toda declared, "The kind of man who makes his wife and children worry cannot do great work in society." Perhaps because my father never caused his family to worry, I wasn't that aware of him when I was young.

In any case, I felt that my future husband not only stood out among others but was also attractive as a trustworthy person with a strong presence.

An excerpt from Mr. Ikeda's memoir published in *Nihon Keizai Shimbun*:

One day in July, I rushed into a member's home to attend a Soka Gakkai meeting. She [Kaneko] was the only one there. Outside, thunder resounded from near and far, but inside the quiet room, silence reigned. Perhaps I should attribute what happened next to my twenty-three-year-old brain cells, but I took a piece of paper lying nearby and penned a verse, which I handed to her. I wrote, "Waiting out the storm,/Fiercely pounds my heart./Is it leaping at the thought of the storm?" I threw myself into writing and remember handing the bit of paper to her, and her wanting to read it right away, though she put it in her handbag when I told her, simply, "No, not now."

The rest of the poem said: "No, I know it beats strongly but only in secret./ Oh, my heart has found/ In you a flowing fountain./ It seeks in you a blossoming flower."

How did you feel after receiving such a romantic poem from the man you so admired?

At that time, I was a young women's group leader in the Soka Gakkai, and I was waiting for people to arrive at a meeting place in Kawasaki City. This is when the poetry incident happened. I had no idea he felt that way. Also, thoughts of marriage had not occurred to me at all.

The poem that he gave me was a love poem, so I was very surprised. Until that time, I had only admired him from afar. After receiving the poem, I began to have feelings for him.

I was surprised, but at that moment, I made up my mind.

Around that time, Daisaku was working for Mr. Toda

at his company in Ichigaya. To get to work, I boarded the train at Yaguchi-no-Watashi, transferred at Kamata and continued on to Yurakucho. That meant we could ride together from Omori Station, where he boarded.

The train was always too crowded for us to talk, so we started to exchange letters.

His love poem was written hastily on the back of a receipt that happened to be at hand. I carried it in my purse for the longest time. Now it's falling apart, but it is still precious to me.

Mr. Ikeda's older brother, Masao, contributed this anecdote:

"I sometimes would see a beautiful young woman on the Mekama train line. Where was she going? I wondered what her family was like. Then Daisaku brought a young woman to our house. I was so surprised because she turned out to be the beautiful young woman that I had noticed on the train."

I sensed that even through his letters, Daisaku sincerely tried to help me develop myself. In matters of faith and in regard to Mr. Toda, there was much that I did not understand at the time. During that period, Daisaku was already aware of his mission in life. He must have kept it all inside. After we married, on the evening of his appointment as president, I told him that his inauguration felt like a funeral to me. By now, that comment seems to have become well known, but again, I believe that I was responding to my husband's feeling [that his new responsibility would require his complete commitment of time and energy].

Mr. Ikeda had this to say about their approaching marriage in his memoir published in the *Nihon Keizai Shimbun*:

"André Maurois states, 'The condition that makes for a successful marriage is to have, during the engagement, the earnest desire to establish a bond that will last forever.' We spoke about facing many hardships together and encouraging each other as we moved forward.

"I asked her things like: There may be times when life is hard, but we must keep going. What if I died young and you were left to raise our children by yourself? Would you be able to handle that? She smiled as she answered: 'I can do it. Everything will be all right.'

"After confirming how we felt about each other, Mr. Toda decided that he would approach our parents to get their support. Summer and autumn had passed, and I remember that it was a cold winter's day."

Please describe the path that led to your marriage.

My husband frequently tells young people, "A marriage is defined not by the mutual admiration two people have when they look into each other's eyes, but rather by the cooperative action they take as they look toward their mutual goals and strive to achieve them."

When we were married, Mr. Toda told us: "When two people are in love and their relationship makes them better people, then that is a good love relationship. If, however, the relationship causes them to ruin their lives, then it is a bad relationship." Mr. Toda's advice to us was quite clear about these kinds of things.

Here is what Fumi Shiraki, a relative, had to say about a conversation she heard between Mr. Toda and Kaneko's mother in the president's office at the Soka Gakkai Headquarters:

"When Mr. Toda said, 'Kaneko found herself an incredible guy, didn't she?' Shizuko, Kaneko's mother, responded, 'Dai-chan [the familiar form of Daisaku] tends to be over the top.'

"Mr. Toda had a good laugh over this comment, and he responded with: 'He may seem like a big talker, but just you wait and see.... He really is quite a guy!' I did not know exactly what Mr. Toda meant, and Shizuko looked totally amazed."

Oh, yes, I recall the anecdote about his being called a "big *furoshiki* (wrapping cloth)," or big talker. I found out much later that my mother had visited Mr. Toda's office. In those days, the youth division was small, and my mother must have been concerned about preventing gossip. She knew that we were seeing each other, but she thought we were much too young for marriage.

When we decided to marry, I was nineteen. When we actually married on May 3, 1952, I had just turned twenty. My mother was the kind of person who always looked forward, so once the decision was made, she stood behind us all the way, especially since Mr. Toda supported our decision.

My mother didn't say anything special to me upon my marriage. All she told me was, "Everything will be all right as long as you practice Buddhism steadfastly and follow President Toda."

How did your husband propose to you?

He simply said, "Put your trust in me and stick with me." As I look back, however, I had been drawn to his humanity, and so I had no other thought in mind than to marry him.

What about him attracted you the most?

I liked the fact that my husband respected and praised his mentor highly. To have served such a distinguished teacher as Mr. Toda since the age of nineteen was Daisaku's greatest source of pride. He would tell me: "It has nothing to do with money or honor. I have met and have been taught by a great mentor, and I feel like the most fortunate person in the world."

You and your husband must have many memories of your experiences with Mr. Toda. Please share one or two with us.

One memory I have is on the occasion of our wedding reception with scores of people attending in a small reception hall. In his celebratory message, Mr. Toda said concisely, "The two of you have pledged yourselves to your faith at a young age, and I hope you will continue to adhere to your faith for as long as you live."

In another memory I hold dear, Mr. Toda declared with tears streaming down his face, "Daisaku may not live past the age of thirty." A few more than ten Soka Gakkai leaders were with him on that occasion, so I heard this story later from my father, who was there. Everyone was surprised at this. It made me think of how great having a mentor is and how strong and deep are the feelings of the mentor toward his disciple. Mr. Toda traveled all over Japan to guide people in their Buddhist faith, and my husband often accompanied him.

When Mr. Toda would leave for rural areas, even if he was embarking from a place like Haneda Airport or Ueno Central Station, I would see him off, taking my children with me, no matter how early in the morning. Then, when he returned to Tokyo, no matter how late, and even if no one else showed up, I would go to welcome him back. Occasionally, two or three Soka Gakkai leaders would go with me. As Mr. Toda's disciples, we continued this practice until his death.

I remember one occasion when Mr. Toda recognized me for this at a meeting by saying, "Kaneko's leadership position in the Soka Gakkai organization may be modest, but I hereby would like to officially appoint her as chief of the hospitality department."

What sort of memorable gifts has your husband given you?

When my husband gave me my wedding ring, he said, "Look, these are diamonds!" Indeed, there were two shiny stones on it. He said, "These symbolize the two of us." Over the years, however, the "diamonds" started to lose their luster.

Later, we found out that they were made of zircon, a crystalline mineral that looks like diamonds. It's a fond memory.

On his first trip to the United States, my husband

brought back a small present for me. This was in October 1960. It was a tiny pill case with jewels like emeralds glittering on the lid. As he handed it to me, he told me, "These are real, and the case was expensive."

It just so happened that, when I went to the United States with him, we found the exact same thing being sold by a vendor at a roadside stall. When I saw it, I exclaimed: "Look! It's one dollar!"

Daisaku burst out laughing. "I've been caught!" he said.

The first time my husband went to the United States, Japanese travelers to the United States were limited to taking thirty-five dollars in currency per person per day. Given this restriction, my husband and those accompanying him did their best to keep their meal expenditures to a minimum so they could use what funds they had left to encourage local members. This is why I feel that this tiny, one-dollar pill case is a priceless expression of his sincerity.

In Mr. Ikeda's novel The Human Revolution, *Josei Toda is quoted as saying at your wedding that Daisaku was like his child, and if Daisaku's bride should be a bad wife who ruins him, Toda would expel her from the organization. He said that he would do all in his power to look out for these two young people and that he wanted them to understand this and accept his best wishes. The text continues, "Toda's words carried with them the affection of a strict father."*

Yes, it was just like that. Up until that point, I rarely had an opportunity to be personally trained or guided by Mr. Toda, and Daisaku played the role of my teacher. At the wedding, Mr. Toda advised me personally. "First, keep your household accounts in order every day.... Second, however badly you may feel, wear a smile on your face when your husband leaves for work in the morning and when he returns in the evening." Fortunately, these admonitions were easy for me to implement.

I have kept a household account ledger and a diary since our marriage. I found that if I neglected to keep the ledger up to date, the items to enter piled up, and it was difficult to remember what they were when trying to enter them later. Also, by keeping the ledger up to date, other benefits accrued.

The household account book had a memo column that I used as a mini-diary. I would write the names of guests who had visited or the cost of train fare, and so on. Later, when my husband went to court, the lawyers had to investigate every little thing. My records were maintained from around 1955, and they gave a thorough description of even the most insignificant expenditures. The lawyers said that they were glad to have this evidence to clearly support the facts.

Of course, my husband was acquitted, and the evidence proved his innocence. From this, I learned that you never know what might come in handy in a pinch.

I used to write brief diary notes in the memo section in the household account book, but after that, I started to write more extensive notes in a yearly notebook. Recently, I have started to use a convenient five-year diary. If I don't write in my diary even for one day, I feel uncomfortable. Even when I go on a trip, I make sure that I write an entry every day.

My five-year diary has the same date for every year on one page. Now, when I tell my husband, "This is what happened last year on this day," or "Two years ago, this is what happened," he seems to think I am quite brilliant.

A long time ago, my husband used to keep a small notebook in which he would always write his schedule. Later, I started keeping his schedule, so I knew at all times where he would be going on any given day or what kind of meeting he was attending.

The novelized version of events following your wedding, as it appears in The Human Revolution, *includes this account: "During the [honeymoon], their conversation centered on resolutions for the future—to respect Mr. Toda as their life-long mentor, never to part from the Soka Gakkai through-out their lives, to contribute to the improvement of society, [and] not to begrudge serving other people."*

My husband talked about our marriage like this: "A husband and wife are one—the man is the legs, and the woman is the body. The man is the arrow, and the woman is the bow. Do you see what I mean?"

"Of course," I agreed. Every marriage is probably

more or less the same, I think. I feel very fortunate that we have lived happily according to our original understanding and mutual agreement. I would not want to look back with any regrets.

We have had to overcome many an obstacle in our lives. My husband always ran full speed ahead, and I have done my best to keep up. So, to tell the truth, there has been little opportunity to look back.

Nevertheless we have not forgotten our beginnings, and no matter how far we have come, we have never lost sight of our common objectives. To maintain the enthusiasm of our youth throughout our lives, we have discovered that mutual encouragement is essential. We are both human, and every human being needs encouragement to thrive.

Please talk about your early married life. I understand that you lived a frugal life in the beginning.

Before we were married, my husband lived in an apartment in Omori called Aobaso. He had been there since May 1949. I was told that it was a two-story apartment complex with three buildings housing ninety families. My husband lived in a small, one-room unit on the first floor.

Since we could hardly live in a one-room apartment, we started our married life in a cousin's rental house in Meguro. Later, the cousin was transferred to Osaka, and he wanted to sell the house, so we found an apartment in the Sanno district of Omori called the Shuzanso Apartments.

Fumi Shiraki had this to say about a visit to the Ikedas' home in Omori:

"A married couple came to the Ikedas' house. It appeared they were having some difficulty with their business. While treating them to dinner, Mr. Ikeda turned toward his wife and remarked: 'We came here with just one pot. Do we still have it?' She answered, 'Yes,' and brought it out to show them.

"It was a well-used pot with lots of dents in it. Mr. Ikeda said: 'We still have it because we want to remember how hard times were when we were first married. That's why it is very precious to us.'

"In the course of the discussion, the couple began to see what he was getting at, naturally, without any special urging. Mr. Ikeda's way of encouraging and counseling really impressed me."

My mother disliked ostentatious displays, so she thought that we should acquire our own household goods rather than have furniture provided by the bride's family, as was traditional. She was a practical woman, and I mean it in the best sense of the word. When my older sister got married, shortages were the rule, so there was no big meal served to the guests at the reception, only bean-paste buns, which were a prized treat in those days.

When I got married, it was not that long after my sister's wedding and the days of shortages, so we got a humble start in our married life as well. It was unthinkable to spend extravagantly on a wedding.

Since I worked at the bank before getting married, I was mindful of finances and naturally refrained from wasteful spending.

I gave most of my wages to my mother, who saved it all for me. Then, when I married, my mother gave me the money she had saved. About six months later, the money from my salary that had been put toward a pension was returned to me. I remember thinking, "This will be the last money that I personally will ever earn." I kept it in a savings account for a long time and later donated it for the construction of the worship hall called Hoan-den at Taiseki-ji temple.

My husband had had a weak constitution since childhood. When we married, he looked like skin and bones. He also had a constant low-grade fever. What's more, after we were married, his schedule was far busier than we ever imagined it would be, and he did not have time to give much thought to taking care of his health.

Mr. Toda advised me, "I want you to take good care of Daisaku." He said: "Health is a priority. Think about health first."

I felt that the most important task I could perform for my husband was to support him quietly from the background so that he could devote himself to his work wholeheartedly and in good health. This became the focus of my life.

A healthy diet is the foundation for a healthy life, so I paid a great deal of attention to our daily diet. My husband was born and raised in what used to be Edo, the oldest and most traditional part of Tokyo, and his parents were engaged in the edible seaweed business. He loved salmon, mackerel, salted squid, *kombu* (edible kelp) and pressed seaweed. He had a habit of eating foods he liked for days on end, so he would eat mackerel, for instance, every day for an entire week. This made it easy on me.

Still, I made sure that he got a balanced diet. My husband would rarely come home in time for dinner, but I made a habit of squeezing vegetables, of which he was not fond, into his late evening snack. He praised the way I glazed the poached mackerel, and he was also fond of a particular crab dish.

My husband always focuses his whole attention—body and soul—on his dialogues and lectures. When they are over, he seems exhausted. After his speaking engagements, I usually give him a massage.

After his resignation (as Soka Gakkai president in April 1979), we were deluged with letters from Soka Gakkai members. I read each one and wrote a response, and my shoulders became stiff from all the writing. I was tapping on my shoulders to relieve the tension, and he quietly came over and massaged my shoulders. That was the first time in thirty years of marriage! I was amazed at the strength in his hands. I had no idea that he was so strong.

When Daisaku was young, he pushed his body beyond

its limits every day. He had adhesions in his lungs, and there was never a day when he woke up in the morning feeling really well. Given that he had been so sickly growing up, his strength was all the more unexpected.

Here is an anecdote from the Ikedas' early days of marriage as recounted by Mr. Ikeda for the *Mainichi Shimbun*, summarized from a column called "My Thoughts":

"Accidentally, the mirror broke on the cosmetic stand that my mother brought in her trousseau when she married. My oldest brother, Kiichi, and I each took one fragment of the broken mirror.

"Before long, Kiichi went off to war and was killed on the battlefront in Burma. I could not help but think that he must have carried that mirror fragment in his breast pocket. I imagined him using it to shave and that it must have brought back to him nostalgic memories of home and his mother. I was using another fragment of the mirror, and I painfully understood how he must have felt. Holding the mirror in my hands brought back thoughts of my brother.

"In 1952, when I married, my wife brought a new mirror stand with her. Now I had a new mirror to use. One day, I came upon my wife with the piece of my mother's mirror in her hand, examining it with a puzzled look. After all, the fragment must have looked like a useless piece of rubbish.

"I suspected that it was destined for the wastebasket, so this is when I first told my wife the history of the mirror fragment and how it related to my mother and to my brother who had died in the war. My wife found a small paulownia box and put the mirror in it. It has been stored there safely ever since."

Do you still have the mirror referred to in your husband's essay "A Piece of Mirror"?

Yes. The piece of mirror is still stored safely in the small paulownia box. The fragment has lots of scratches, so at first I wondered why he wanted to keep such a thing. I thought there must be a reason. He kept it safe all through the war, and after the war, when he lived at the Aobaso Apartments, he kept it in his desk drawer and took good care of it.

In his essay, my husband describes in detail the history related to the mirror, but when he told me about it, he did not discuss it as thoroughly. Still, the moment he said, "My mother's mirror has been watching over me," I thought to myself, "This is a person who has experienced more than the ordinary person's share of hardships." For the first time, I could sense what it meant to him.

After beginning to study under Mr. Toda, my husband rarely had an opportunity to visit his parents. It must have been hard for him, since he had such deep affection for his mother and father. In his young mind, however, he had determined to persevere because he felt that his efforts would ultimately benefit his parents.

The essay explained that, by looking in the mirror fragment, the young Ikeda realized that his health was suffering and that he should pay attention to his diet. On the other hand, when he felt happy, he could see it in his face, and this would make him start whistling. When he saw himself in the morning as he was combing his hair, he said the mirror would remind him of his mother's quiet way of showing her concern for him, and he would whisper to himself, "Good morning, Mother."

The essay includes a similar anecdote about Mr. Toda, who received a light coat known as an *atsushi* from his mother when he left his hometown to make a living elsewhere. Mr. Toda kept the coat, made by hand with painstaking effort and loving care, with him throughout his life. It survived the fires of war. Mr. Toda was fond of saying, "As long as I have this *atsushi* with me, I will be safe."

I have a strong sense that my husband must have regarded the mirror in the same way.

3

Building a Happy Home

A YOUNG MAN filled with aspirations and a young woman who cheers him on—what kind of home will the couple create? This chapter explores the Ikeda household's approach to family and education.

Kaneko was married at twenty. She gave birth to her first son, Hiromasa, at twenty-one; her second son, Shirohisa, at twenty-two; and her third son, Takahiro, at twenty-six. She became the mother of three boys, and two years later, when her husband became president of the Soka Gakkai, she became the wife of the president at the young age of twenty-eight.

The Ikeda household was, in a sense, a workplace where people continually gathered. Mrs. Ikeda saw her role as a wife as follows: "I felt that the most important task I could perform for my husband was to support him quietly from the background so that he could devote himself to his work wholeheartedly and in good health. This became the focus of my life."

Her words conjure up the image of a housewife from the olden days. Mrs. Ikeda, however, was more than just another

docile wife. Because her husband's schedule was always packed
and he tended to be away often, it fell to her to raise three sons
while giving them a strong sense of their father's presence.
One day, a schoolteacher paid a routine visit to the Ikeda
home. He asked the boys what they wanted to be when they
grew up. All three sons immediately declared, "I want to be
like my father." Mrs. Ikeda was thirty-two and Mr. Ikeda
thirty-six at the time. Mrs. Ikeda says, "It all comes down to
what example the parents choose to set for their children."

The Ikeda household observed four rules, which will be
introduced in this chapter, the impact of which extends far
beyond the family's personal happiness. Each one has been
and still is an integral, continuous part of the Ikeda family's
way of life from the early days of their marriage.

*What kind of place did you live in when you were first
married?*

In August 1952, we moved to the Shuzanso Apartments in
the Omori Sanno area of Tokyo, about a ten-minute walk
from Omori Station. It was a two-story building with a red
roof, and ten families lived there. Our home was on the
first floor and had a four-tatami-mat Japanese-style room,
a six-mat Western-style room, and a one-half-mat kitchen
(each tatami was about 35.5 by 71 inches). The laundry
space and toilets were shared with the other families. There
was no washing machine, and in those days everyone went
to the public bathhouse, so there was no bath.

After we moved in, we immediately set up our altar and started chanting and reciting the sutra rather loudly. This upset the landlord, who cautioned us by saying, "If people hear chanting coming from the apartment, they won't want to live here."

We had a bookshelf in the Western-style room with a wooden floor. My husband would sometimes buy used books. Once he brought home used books that were infested with bedbugs.

The next morning, my husband said he felt itchy. I asked my mother what to do, and she instructed us to spray the books and all the rooms with insecticide.

January 1953 was our first New Year's holiday at the Shuzanso Apartments. Our youth division colleagues came to our home. Just seven people filled the room to overflowing. Despite our tiny kitchen, we prepared suki-yaki and did our best to extend our hospitality.

On that occasion, my husband took a book from the shelf—a poetry collection by Bansui Doi—and read aloud the poem "A Star Falls in the Autumn Wind on Wuzhang Plains." It was a poem expressing the feelings of Zhuge Liang, the hero of Romance of the Three Kingdoms, in his later years. One member of the group knew the song that was based on the poem, and everyone agreed that both the poem and the song were wonderful.

My husband suggested that we all perform it for Mr. Toda. The very next day, we all went to sing for Mr. Toda. He was so thrilled that he kept saying, with tears streaming down his face, "Would you sing it again, please?"

After that, the song became a Soka Gakkai favorite and was sung far and wide. Its popularity began in our small home, something that moves me deeply when I look back on those days.

Please share your recollections of the time you became a mother.

Hiromasa was born on April 28, 1953, a year after we were married. When we married, my husband was twenty-four and I was only twenty. I became a mother when I was twenty-one years old. I was probably a little young for motherhood.

Actually, my husband was in a position of some responsibility as head of the sales department in Mr. Toda's company. Because of Daisaku's weak constitution, Mr. Toda urged him to "hurry up and settle down." Mr. Toda believed Daisaku would be better off having someone to look after his health. It also meant Daisaku could more freely devote himself to his work.

When our first child was born, Daisaku was in Fujinomiya in Shizuoka, holding a Soka Gakkai event with Mr. Toda in celebration of the seven-hundredth anniversary of the establishment of Nichiren Buddhism. About eight hundred men from the youth division gathered to mark the event in grand style. As it happened, our son was born on the day of the event. My husband was delighted. News of the birth had already reached Mr. Toda, and he composed a poem and sent it to me.

The poem, which Mr. Toda wrote on a folding fan, read: "A spring moon / Shares my delight / At the birth of your child." My husband told me that the poem was written on the fan that Mr. Toda had been using at the ceremony.

When he was around one or two, Hiromasa learned how to put records on the phonograph. I worried that he would scratch the records and ruin them, so I hid them under the desk. It never occurred to me that the hiding place I chose was right at child's-eye level, completely visible to him.

He would easily slip under the desk to get them. I had to be amused. We are often encouraged to view things through the eyes of a child, and this convinced me of the wisdom of that advice.

One day, my husband told me that he would buy me some clothes when we were at a store near Omori Station. This was the first time he had ever said anything like this. He was saying, "Let's get this, this, this, this, and this one, too," all the while picking out blouses.

I preferred to shop a little more discriminatingly. Besides, I knew how much money he had in his wallet, so I told him, "Just one will be fine."

He looked up at me and said, "You don't seem very happy at all!" *[Kaneko laughs at this recollection.]*

Managing the household budget was extremely challenging, and this period was probably the most difficult.

The first rule of household management is to value things and never waste them. We did not waste even one grain of rice. I never threw away leftovers but rather figured out how to include them in the next meal. We recycled wrapping paper, folding it neatly to use again. Even a piece of string was used over and over again. We did our best to be frugal because we had experienced harsh times during the war.

On March 30, 1954, my husband was made chief of the youth division general staff, a newly established position, and so he was busy every day traveling around the country. Shirohisa was born on January 28, 1955, one year and eight months after our first son. Hiromasa was a big baby, but Shirohisa was small at birth. He grew quickly on his own.

When Shirohisa was born, there was no floor space for a baby bed, so at times we had to make a bed for him on top of the baby dresser.

Since Hiromasa was a restless sleeper, moving this way and that, it was probably safer for Shirohisa up there.

We lived in the Shuzanso Apartments for approximately three years. I got to know a woman who lived on the second floor who also had a baby. We would see each other in the laundry room when we were washing diapers. Several years ago, I received a letter from her. I was so happy to hear from her; it made me nostalgic about those days. I had forgotten and was surprised that she remembered that I had given her some of our children's toys when we moved. I learned that her husband, who had worked for a trading company, had died, so my husband and I offered our prayers for him. Every encounter is so very precious.

At that time, my mother babysat for us a lot. She also attended Soka Gakkai meetings, so our oldest son bounced back and forth like a rubber ball between our home and my parents' home. Both my mother and I would take Hiromasa walking. He would toddle after us, doing his best to keep up. It became part of our daily routine, and he came to like being outdoors. He was a healthy child and seldom got sick or injured.

According to the rules at the Shuzanso Apartments, families could only have one child. So, in June 1955, after Shirohisa was born, we moved into a one-story house in Kobayashi-cho close to my parents. In the beginning, there were two six-tatami-mat rooms and one four-and-a-half-mat room. Over time, it became cramped, so we added another six-mat room. Stories about our Kobayashi-cho period appear in my husband's book *A Youthful Diary*. He frequently wrote, "My wife came to the train station to meet me." On his return to town, he would call home and I would arrange to meet him when he arrived at Kamata Station. In the mornings, he would ride his bicycle to the station, so on the way home, he and I would take turns pushing the bicycle as we walked. It was about a fifteen-minute walk.

I was always concerned that my husband was so exhausted. In fact, that was an indication of how poor his health was at the time. In the winter, he would break out in night sweats, and in the mornings, his face would be bright red.

I believe that his constant low-grade fever was likely

the cause, not his feverish passion for his work and mission in life.

Often, when he was returning from Osaka on the night train, he would arrive in Tokyo in the morning and then go directly to the Soka Gakkai Headquarters. Of course I was worried about him, and although it was difficult with small children, I would take them with me to meet his train at Tokyo Station and give him a change of clothes. I perceived my mission in life to be taking care of my husband's health. I can hardly believe how healthy he seems these days compared to back then. For me, my husband's good health is my greatest happiness.

Eiko Akiyama, SGI general women's leader, contributes this anecdote about the Ikedas' early home life:

"When I would visit the Ikedas' home in those days, I was struck by how modestly they lived. In his role as a youth division leader, Mr. Ikeda always seemed so well organized and dignified. The frugality of his home life posed a striking contrast to my first impressions.

"When I met his wife, she was so kind and charming. She impressed me as a truly wonderful wife. After that, I would visit occasionally. One day, when I came to visit, Mrs. Ikeda was wearing a kimono. Mr. Ikeda asked me: 'Don't you think she looks nice in a kimono? How much do you think it cost?' Then he told me that the material was synthetic and added, 'She's good at stretching her budget.' Mrs. Ikeda flashed me a grin.

"When I would come to visit, Mr. Ikeda would tell his wife:

'Please bring something to eat. I'm sure she's hungry.' In those days, food was scarce. I remember once she brought out some slightly green tomatoes. Mr. Ikeda teased her gently, saying, 'I've always told you that we should be prepared when youth division members come over.' When she left the room, Mr. Ikeda leaned toward me and whispered: 'We don't have anything. Nothing. If we did, she would bring it all out.' That brought a lump to my throat."

I heard there is an essay titled "Big Three Summit" with your sons as its theme.

After my third son, Takahiro, was born on April 11, 1958, I had three growing boys. My oldest son, the elder statesman, was a scholarly type. The middle leader was the most overweight child in his class and was nicknamed "Taiho" after a famous sumo wrestler. The youngest leader was a mama's boy who was nicknamed "Mini-tank" for being so agile and quick. Throughout the year, one could hear "Bam!" "Thud!" and other sounds coming from the house.

In the evening, the three boys would enjoy taking their bath together. They would raise a ruckus and, on two occasions, broke the bottom of the wooden bathtub. My husband observed in his essay that they must have needed to live up to their reputation as "Sons of the Sea" [a reference to Japan as a sea nation].

How Mrs. Ikeda dealt with her children is reflected in this anecdote told by the manager of a Soka Gakkai community center near the Ikeda home:

"When Takahiro was small, he burst out crying one day as Mrs. Ikeda was leaving to go to a meeting. He didn't usually run after her when she was leaving, but he must have felt different that day. Two days later, I saw Mrs. Ikeda talking to Takahiro. They were discussing the pros and cons of some decision, and although I didn't catch the gist of the entire conversation, what impressed me was the way Mrs. Ikeda conversed with the child, giving him respect as both an individual and a rational person. She always spoke to him in this manner."

The family's housekeeper added this observation:

"Mrs. Ikeda is very good at instantly changing her focus. For example, before Mr. Ikeda returns home, she has dinner with her children and then she and the children do their evening prayers together. Mother and children interact in a pleasant way. She listens to them attentively, nodding her head and praising them. They seem to enjoy this peaceful and happy time together.

"Then, when Mr. Ikeda comes home, Mrs. Ikeda immediately shifts her focus. At that moment, she places all her attention on him. When she speaks to Mr. Ikeda about the children, she again becomes very much the mother.

"After I myself started a family and had a child, I would always look back and realize how much I learned from her. Whether I can put those lessons into practice is the 'homework' that remains for me, but I've learned from Mrs. Ikeda about the joys of doing one's best. "

~~~~~~   ▦

When the children were small, they seemed to know that when their father returned home, they shouldn't compete for my attention. I am fully aware of my husband's busy schedule and do my best to give him every opportunity to relax.

Just as when I was a child, our household treats our morning and evening prayers seriously. When my husband is home, we chant as a family. When he is away, I take the lead. From watching my husband chanting, I learned a lot and know the value of morning and evening prayers.

At the same time, if I had been overly strict about it, the children might have grown to dislike the practice. My husband says it all depends on the mother's faith. We customarily gathered at 7:00 AM to chant. If one child was absent, I'd ring the bell and call out, "It's time for morning prayers." As a rule, this brought everyone together. It did happen, though, that one child or another might oversleep and have to leave home without doing his morning prayers. I felt that admonishing them as they were leaving for school would be counterproductive. It is better for a child to be sent off with a smile and a cheerful word first thing in the morning.

Mr. Toda urged me to send off and greet my husband with a smile each day, and I believe that his advice also applies to the children. Boys are especially difficult because they tend to have a prickly sense of pride. Mr. Toda advised, "However badly you may feel, wear a smile." If, for some reason, it was not possible for one of the children to chant in the morning, I would say: "Don't worry. I will chant for you." It seems to have worked.

Once, when Takahiro was in high school, he planned to go to Ogasawara with his astronomy club to observe the stars. The date overlapped with a meeting of the Soka Gakkai's future division, the group for children up to high-school age, and I told him he should attend the meeting. Takahiro insisted that he couldn't back out of the trip with his friends since it had been planned for a long time. I consulted my husband, who advised: "Faith is for a lifetime and, taking the long view, wouldn't it be better to let him go to Ogasawara this time? What is most important, after all, is that he continues practicing." I felt such a sense of relief when he said that.

A woman who participated in Soka Gakkai activities with Mrs. Ikeda in the Kobayashi-cho days shared this story of Mrs. Ikeda and her children:

"Mrs. Ikeda often said: 'A mother must first of all pray earnestly for her children. Meetings are educational venues, so take children to meetings without hesitation.'

"I will never forget the image of her eldest son sitting quietly by her side as Mrs. Ikeda lectured on Nichiren's writings. As they sat facing the Gohonzon, she would tell him, 'Today's meeting is very important.'

"When I asked her, 'Will such a small child understand what you are telling him?' she said: 'Of course. We are communicating on a life-to-life basis.'

"One time, her oldest son was happily playing with a toy sword, waving it all around as he said, 'Papa bought this for me.' He accidentally hit his mother's hand with it, causing her finger to bleed.

"Mrs. Ikeda stopped Hiromasa, pointing out to him: 'You made Mama bleed. That's not why Papa bought you your toy.'

"Regarding the practice of reciting portions of the Lotus Sutra, Mrs. Ikeda said: 'You must not force a child to sit and chant if he or she is not so inclined. Instead, help the child to grow and develop naturally.'"

I handled sibling fights by telling the boys, "As an older brother, you must take good care of your younger brother." And to the younger one, "A younger brother should respect his older brother."

There is a saying that the character a child has at age three will last a hundred years. The saying can be taken in both positive and negative ways. Buddhism teaches that we should not center our lives on our personal benefit alone but should aspire to the service of others, too. The "human revolution" spoken of in the Soka Gakkai is one manifestation of this way of thinking. Children, too, should be urged in that direction from early on; there are many golden opportunities to encourage them. It would be best if not only mothers but fathers also would take advantage of these opportunities, but usually mothers have the most contact with their children. If, for example, a squabble starts between two siblings, a mother can skillfully reason with the children so they will gradually understand how to relate to each other.

I have come to believe that the mother herself must also grow and develop. If she does not, then the children will not develop in the true sense of the word, either.

Fumi Shiraki had this to say about the boys:

"I understand that when the children were small, they were well-behaved and did not roughhouse or carelessly break things, not even tearing the paper on the sliding doors and screens in the house.

"One day, Shirohisa was playing with a toy, and his younger brother, Takahiro, said, 'I wish you would let me play with that.' I think most boys would have just fought over the toy, but Takahiro, his eyes spilling over with tears, just asked to be allowed to play with it. I was impressed that he could express his wishes so clearly."

Did the Ikeda family have house rules?

We did not have house rules as such, but we always stressed the following points:
1. Live for the welfare of others and of society.
2. Relate honestly with all people.
3. Maintain your faith and conviction throughout life.
4. More important than winning is to not be defeated. That way, you will ultimately win in everything.

It is often said that children grow up watching their parents and imitating their behavior. It all comes down to what example the parents choose to set for their children.

The most important aspect of a father's role is to not disillusion the child but always to give him or her dreams and hope. This is easy to say but actually very hard to do.

My husband was certainly always busy, but his fondness for the children was always apparent. When I talked about the children, the stern expression on his face would soften, and he would break into a happy smile. When he would return home so exhausted that he could barely respond to me, suddenly he would ask about the children.

I would wonder if he had really been listening to what I just told him. However, I would let it pass.

He enjoyed playing with the children, and even after he was appointed president, whenever he had time, he would play games with them like sumo or scooping goldfish out of the water with a net.

The education of the children, however, was left mostly to me, although I consulted my husband about important decisions. I tried as much as possible not to trouble him with unnecessary details. He would say: "It is better to leave the education of the children to their mother. No matter how much a mother scolds the children, they will not become bitter or resentful. But if the father harasses and scolds them, their development will surely be warped." This is something he learned from Mr. Toda.

My husband never became angry with the children. He would let them be as free as possible. He said he wanted them to grow up healthy, as straight and upright as bamboo, so they could make their own unique and valuable contributions to society. This does not mean focusing merely on achieving success or prominence. He wanted the children to become people who would be of service to society.

When my husband traveled abroad or to other prefectures, sometimes he would be home only for a few months out of the year. In the course of his travels, we would occasionally receive a phone call from him. The boys would take turns chatting with their father about what kind of souvenirs they wanted him to bring back and other small talk. They seemed to be used to their father being away all the time, but they were, after all, lonely for him.

He would send each of them letters and postcards from abroad, usually covered with lots of stamps. Still, I was extremely concerned about how the boys perceived their father.

One day, when one of their schoolteachers was visiting, he asked the children what they wanted to be when they grew up. All the boys said without missing a beat, "I want to be like my father." Tears welled up in my eyes.

Since my children became adults, I have asked them to live with integrity and sincerity. All I have wanted is for them to live fully and to remain unshaken by the shallow, superficial things of this world; to lead lives based on profound principles. I wanted them to set their hearts on taking an honest path and to live full and meaningful lives. I am thankful that these hopes have been fulfilled.

Here is a memory contributed by one of Mrs. Ikeda's neighbors in Shinano-machi when they first moved there in 1966:

"One thing about Mrs. Ikeda that made a lasting impression on me was the way she sent off Takahiro, her third son, every morning. I think the boy was in second grade at the time. With his satchel on his back, the little boy would take off down the hill and around the corner at the bottom, all the while waving to his mother. And she would wave back until he was out of sight around the bend.

"I didn't think it was possible to go to this extent every day. But this image of Mrs. Ikeda, comfortable in her role as mother, still remains in my mind. It made me realize that everyday acts are so important in raising children."

~~~~~~ ▨

I approach most things in life according to their degree of necessity. If I feel that I should be doing something, then it gets done with one step naturally following the next. That's about how it works. There is no need to make things more complicated than they need to be.

If I put myself in another person's shoes, I can see things quite clearly.

People try to behave toward others as they would like to be treated themselves. On the other hand, if one is injured by someone and then tries to pass that on to others, what will happen? There will be no progress and no improvement.

▨ ~~~~~~~~~~~~~~~~~~~~~~~~~~~~~~~~~~~~~~~

An essay by Mr. Ikeda in *Sankei Shimbun* tells about an evening when he came home early for the first time in a long while. The boys called him into the living room, where he noticed something different — a sheet hanging from the wall by string and decorated with a ribbon on each side. The three boys had planned a welcome-home and thank-you party for their father that featured an eight-millimeter film. The essay continues:

"The ribbons looked like something that came off a package. The boys seemed a little bashful about the quickly assembled production, but I thought it was heartwarming and cute. The light was turned off, and the children's masterpieces were shown on the screen one after another. As we watched, my impression of the ribbons stuck in the back of my mind. Afterward, I found out that the movie night was the children's suggestion, but the ribbons were my wife's idea."

There is more.

"Even if there is little time for the entire family to spend together, families that create memories are creating experiences for their children that are more valuable than riches. Even a short space of time can be made many times more precious.

"If there is no sense of value creation in the family, then there is no joy. This is something completely different from an abundance of material things. It might be called a richness of the heart."

My husband and I both agree that we live in an age with an overabundance of material things. We hear stories about families who have gotten into trouble. For instance, imagine the members of a family living beyond their means and accumulating credit card debt. Then, having created a certain lifestyle, they try to maintain the image of wealth by spending more extravagantly, which exacerbates the problem. Next, the situation becomes a source of contention between husband and wife, and the family begins to live under a dark and gloomy cloud. The lengthy recession in Japan has put added pressure on household budgets, but even if family members can afford luxuries, if they do not have the capacity to think of others, they are impoverished at heart.

Of the greatest concern is how the hearts of adults who lack the capacity to care for others are reflected in their children.

If parents are overly competitive and thus their children become too competitive, and that competitiveness turns to the acquisition of money and material goods, then what kind of future will the children have? We, as adults, must think about this very seriously.

The following comment is from Kaneko's sister-in-law, Miyoko Shiraki.

"Gardenias bloom prolifically in their garden, and bugs seem to be very attracted to the flowers. When I fling open the door to the yard and see bugs on the flowers, I close the door right away.

"One day, Kaneko cut a whole bucketful of gardenia blossoms and washed them, petals, stalks, branches, and leaves. Then she decorated the entire house with gardenias. They had such a wonderful fragrance. It was a small thing, but it made such a big difference in the ambience of the house. She rearranged this picture or moved that ornament from one place to the other, decorated with flowers, and put some thought into beautifying the entire house so that, when her husband came home, it seemed like a totally different place.

Kaneko Ikeda with her husband, SGI President Daisaku Ikeda, in Nagano, August 2004. *(Photo credit: Hiromasa Ikeda)*

Kaneko, age 4, at home with her older brother,
Fumio.

The Shiraki family at home in Yaguchi-no-Watashi, Tokyo. (Clockwise from left) Kaneko Shiraki's younger brother, Shuji, in the arms of his father, Shigeji; Kaneko's mother, Shizuko; Kaneko's older sister, Yoshi; Kaneko, age 5; and Kaneko's older brother, Fumio.

Kaneko, age 10, with her younger brother, Shuji.

Kaneko (third row, center), a fourth-grade student at Yaguchi
Elementary School, during an excursion to Inokashira Park
in Musashino City, Tokyo.

Kaneko, age 16 or 17, at home when she was a student at Chofu Academy.

Kaneko (back row, center) at a Chofu Academy culture festival,
November 1946.

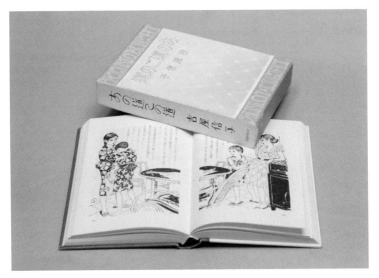

One of young Kaneko's favorite books, *That Road, This Road*.

賞状

白木かね

人トナリ温厚篤實ニシテ表裏ナク連年学
級委話係ニ選バレテ級務ニ勵ミ指導統率
宜シキニ適ヒ學友ノ信望ヲ蒐ム又入學以来
終始一貫眞摯ナル態度ヲ以テ精進ノ道ニ
勵ミテ息マズノ温和ナル風格ハ自ラ他ニ推重
スル所トナル學業成績亦優秀ナリ仍テ茲ニ
之ヲ賞ス

第八號

昭和廿五年三月廿五日

調布高等學校長　西村一郎

Character award presented to Kaneko during her Chofu
Academy days.

Kaneko (third row, seventh from left) during the
Chofu Academy graduation ceremony, March 1950.

Second Soka Gakkai president Josei Toda
giving a lecture.

Left: The first Soka Gakkai Headquarters in Nishi-Kanda, Tokyo.

Below: Aobaso Apartments, where Daisaku Ikeda lived before his marriage.

Daisaku and Kaneko Ikeda on their wedding day, May 3, 1952.

The *Gosho Zenshu* (The Collected Writings of Nichiren Daishonin) presented to Kaneko by Josei Toda. He inscribed the following: "May your gentle image in the moonlight / be filled with the strength of the Mystic Law. / Josei / To Kane Ikeda."

Kaneko's wedding ring.

Newlyweds Daisaku and Kaneko.

The pillbox that Daisaku gave
to Kaneko as a souvenir
from the United States.
(Illustration by Kaoru Miki)

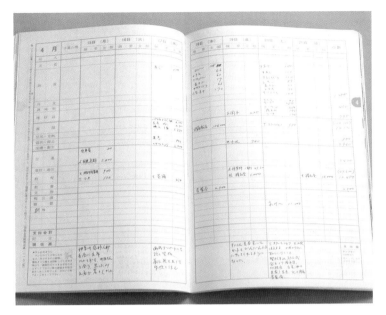

Financial records Kaneko kept for her family.

An abacus and
hotplate used by
Kaneko early
in her marriage.

Kaneko (center) with Daisaku, Hiromasa, and her mother, Shizuko, aboard a train to Fujinomiya, Shizuoka, July 1953.

Kaneko and Daisaku, 1954.

"When Mr. Ikeda opened the door, there was Kaneko, sitting very properly, waiting for him. On her face was a smile beautiful beyond words, and her manner was so natural. She greeted her husband smiling joyfully, and he was thrilled and relaxed to be at home. Sometimes Kaneko would wear a kimono, or in summer, a *yukata* (light summer kimono). Japanese-style clothing becomes her, and Mr. Ikeda would tell her, 'You look great.'"

My life consisted of waking up every morning and looking at my husband's face because I was worried about his health. His daily activities were often stressful, so at least when he was home, I wanted him to relax and rest both his body and his mind. For that reason, I did everything I could, including decorating with flowers and sometimes wearing a kimono, to help him relax when he stepped through the door.

I never permitted my sons any special treatment. We are common, ordinary people just like everyone else. That's how I wanted my sons to be treated. Their allowances were no more than average for their age, and if they ever wanted to buy anything that cost more than that, they got part-time jobs to earn the money. Their part-time jobs were good experiences for them.

Since my husband was not often at home, he had little direct involvement with the children's studies. To compensate, he would always give them things like books or fountain pens for their birthdays. He chose presents that related to their studies. Because he was so busy, however,

I was the one who actually purchased the presents he'd chosen. I would hide them, and then when he returned home, they would be available at the right time for my husband to give them to the children. My husband liked to indulge the children and, without hesitation, promised them things. He would tell me what he had promised, and I would get the items and put them on each child's desk at the appropriate time. This was one of the ways that I helped the children bond with their father and raise points for my husband.

Were both you and your husband passionate about
your children's formal education and school entrance
examinations?

I was not one of those education-obsessed mothers. I never nagged my children to study. Instead, I raised my children so that each could follow his own interests and forge his own path in life.

Hiromasa was the kind of child who didn't have to be reminded to study. Shirohisa was able to get by, even though he didn't study very much. Takahiro was totally absorbed in astronomy rather than his schoolwork. He wholeheartedly pursued his hobby—he would rather research the Milky Way than do his schoolwork. I was not overly concerned about the children's homework, and that is probably because I am an optimist at heart.

Takahiro had a tutor at one time who came to the

house. Part of the reason for hiring a tutor was my husband's wish to help the tutor, a student who was struggling financially, to continue his own studies. But the tutor was stymied, in the same way I was, by Takahiro's nimble brain.

Takahiro got the tutor to join him in activities that wouldn't fit the usual definition of "study." I'd hear banging and slamming, and Takahiro would be on the tutor's back, for example, getting a horseback ride. They'd have a great time right until dinner at the end of the day. It was always like that.

Even so, this relationship was a good influence on Takahiro.

When the children were approaching the age at which they would take their college entrance exams, I wanted at least one of them to go to Soka University, the university their father had founded.

Hiromasa had attended Keio Junior and Senior High School and so continued on to Keio University. We respected our children's wishes to the highest degree, but I did have my preferences. Shirohisa went to Seikei Academy during junior and senior high school, after which he wanted to attend a pharmaceutical college. He had made up his mind and would not change it.

When I found out that Shirohisa wanted to study pharmacology, I was astonished. I remembered that, just before I graduated from my girls' high school, when I agonized over whether to pursue higher education, I thought that I wanted to serve in the health field by studying pharmacology. I was now surprised that my son had the same interest.

Ever since elementary school, Shirohisa had been a large child and liked things that were big and stood out. On the other hand, he was also sensitive and considerate of others. Since it was what he wanted, I respected his wishes to take the exams for the college of his choice. Even so, I still hoped he would go to Soka University, and so I prayed for this.

Later, Shirohisa changed his mind about his plans. When the time came to take the college entrance exams, he opted to also take the Soka University exam. He went to the campus for the exam and decided that he liked it. Although he still seemed a bit reluctant in his decision, he entered Soka University. I was thrilled.

Takahiro had attended Keio schools from elementary school, so he continued on to Keio University. Later on, in order to achieve his dream of becoming an elementary school teacher, he decided to transfer to the education department at Soka University. Perhaps his brother, who was attending Soka University, had some influence on him.

When Shirohisa was small, he caught a terrible cold. At that time, Daisaku asked me how I was praying. I told him that I was praying that my son's cold not become too serious, but my husband said, "You should pray for him to never catch a cold." In this way, he taught me how to approach prayer. His chanting of Nam-myoho-renge-kyo was focused and to the point; nothing was wasted. Once, when I said, "I intend to win," he told me, "Don't say 'intend'; say that you *will* win." When it came to matters of faith, he was strict.

Therefore, when I prayed for my children's safety, I prayed that they would never have an accident. Aware of our responsibility in the Soka Gakkai, the children themselves, I believe, took special care to avoid accidents.

Hiromasa was the last one among his college friends to get his driver's license. He obtained his license when he was a senior in college. Until then, he commuted to the university by bicycle. I told him that it was more dangerous to go by bicycle, but he insisted: "If I have an accident on my bicycle, then I am the only one who will get hurt. But if I have an accident while driving, then the other party will be injured. That's why I don't want to drive."

I finally persuaded him to get his license by saying: "But if you get hurt, many Soka Gakkai members will be worried about you and it will be a problem for everyone. If you just drive carefully, everything should be all right." Hiromasa was the firstborn son, so perhaps it was inevitable, a matter of destiny, that he felt a particularly heavy sense of responsibility. My third son got his license as soon as he graduated from high school. We left the decision up to him.

To illustrate Mrs. Ikeda's "optimist at heart" approach to life, a housekeeper in the Ikeda home recounted a story about Takahiro from his college days.

"One evening, it was getting quite late, but Takahiro still had not returned home. Even after Mr. Ikeda came home, there was still no sign of Takahiro. Mr. Ikeda seemed worried, but Mrs. Ikeda was very calm.

"After some time had passed, Mr. Ikeda said to her, 'What about Takahiro?'

"She replied: 'He's probably still on the ocean. Isn't it better for him to be out boating with his friends than to be playing around downtown somewhere?'"

Of course, I was worried that he might have had an accident. But as we went through experiences like that, our children gradually became independent.

4

Living with a Trailblazing Husband

MAY 3, 1960—the day Mr. Ikeda was inaugurated president of the Soka Gakkai—was an unforgettable day for Mrs. Ikeda. As she reflects: "That day marked a shift in the proportion of our lives that was public versus private. Our visibility in the public arena gradually increased."

Mr. Ikeda became much busier, especially with communications and reports streaming in constantly from around the entire world. His health, however, was not good. Mrs. Ikeda's life changed dramatically as well when, in the winter of 1969, Mr. Ikeda became sick during his travels. In response to his doctor's strong request, Mrs. Ikeda began accompanying her husband when he attended events around Japan. Since the autumn of 1964, Mrs. Ikeda has traveled with her husband on overseas trips, starting with his round of visits to Southeast Asia, the Middle East, and Europe. Because of uncertain health demonstrated by Mr. Ikeda's collapse during a trip to the United States, the executive staff of the Soka Gakkai requested that his wife accompany him on all overseas trips.

In the midst of this busy life, Mrs. Ikeda continued to

manage her own affairs successfully. Her cheerfulness, even when facing great difficulty, was a boon to the family. No matter what happened, she never faltered. But she admits, "When I accompanied him, I would also get extremely tired and once got very sick." That was in the fall of 1975. For a while, when Mr. Ikeda arrived home late at night, she let him have the bedroom to himself in order to give him a chance to sleep soundly. It shows just how exhausting their daily life had become. Here, though, Mrs. Ikeda's exceptionally positive attitude can be seen. She said that, having become ill herself, she experienced for the first time the difficulties that her husband faced.

That she spoke frankly caused her husband a bit of apprehension on their first trip to China in 1974. Her honesty, however, served to deepen the relationships of trust with their Chinese hosts. This kind of courage, to state things just as they are, seems very characteristic of Mrs. Ikeda, and her husband may have sighed with relief at the outcome.

By traveling as a couple and meeting with such esteemed figures as British historian Arnold Toynbee and his wife, and China's Prime Minister Zhou Enlai and his wife, Mr. and Mrs. Ikeda have pioneered a new kind of diplomacy, developing genuine friendships through visiting with and getting to know foreign dignitaries and their families.

Mr. Ikeda's book *A Youthful Diary* contains the following passage:

"At last, Mr. Toda has become president [of the Soka Gakkai]. This was the long-awaited, common wish of all his disciples. I will remember this day for the rest of my life." (*A Youthful Diary*, p. 110)

Mr. Ikeda was a youth of twenty-three at the time. In his diary entry for January 6, 1951, he writes:

"Helped with various matters all evening at [Josei Toda's] house…. I keenly sense his extraordinary resolve. Mr. Toda is like Masashige [a fourteenth-century samurai considered to personify the virtues of courage and loyalty], while I am like Masatsura [his son, who supported Masashige in his struggles]. His wife wept. Never throughout my life will I forget the emotion, solemnity, tears, sense of mission, of karmic bonds and of life's worth that I have experienced today. It has been decided that I will be his successor. (*A Youthful Diary*, p. 73)

Even after our marriage, I was not privy to any private discussions before the recommendation and appointment of my husband as president of the organization. My husband didn't tell me anything about it. After we began seeing each other, I did , in my own way, become aware of the sense of mission my husband felt as a direct disciple of Josei Toda.

■ ~~~~~~

Here is Fumi Shiraki's recollection of Mr. Ikeda's inauguration:

"After the general meeting at which Mr. Ikeda was appointed the third president of the Soka Gakkai, my husband and I went to the Ikedas' residence in Kobayashi-cho to pay our respects. The entryway had been freshly sprinkled with water, and I still remember how it glistened brightly in the sunlight.

"As we stepped into the entryway, my husband called out: 'Good evening! It's Giichiro.'

"'Come on in,' Mr. Ikeda said in a friendly and welcoming voice, and so we went into the house. We immediately noticed that the mood in the room was completely different from the usual ambience. Mrs. Ikeda seemed so grave and somber. Mr. Ikeda explained: 'She didn't make any *sekihan* (celebratory red rice and beans) for me. She says that today we are observing a funeral.'"

~~~~~~ ■

May 3, 1960, was the most unforgettable day of my life. My husband was inaugurated president of the Soka Gakkai. Our normal family life ended on that day. The next day, my husband would become a public person who would work for the benefit of all people. This was my husband's mission in life. No one else could do the work that he had to do, so I felt that I must do my utmost to make sure that he could wholeheartedly devote all his energy to his work. I made up my mind that I would be strong and withstand whatever storms might come.

I was unable to feel joyful about the appointment of my husband to the presidency of the Soka Gakkai. It felt like a funeral to me, and this expressed my true feelings. That day marked the beginning of a new life in which our public lives would gradually begin to overtake our private lives.

A housekeeper in the Ikeda home shares her observations:

"The year 1969 was what they call an unlucky year for Daisaku Ikeda, according to the Chinese calendar. That was the year his health suffered from overwork. He had a constant low-grade fever, and it was a very difficult time. Mrs. Ikeda, however, remained calm and composed and did not change the manner in which she interacted with the children. I was completely amazed at the prompt and efficient way that she managed everything. I would be hard pressed to emulate her example."

In the summer of 1969, my husband put all his energy into the summer training course and lecture session held over several days for one hundred thousand people. He became so exhausted that winter from traveling around the Kansai and Chubu regions to encourage people in their Buddhist activities that he caught a severe cold, which turned into pneumonia.

When my husband was in Osaka, he had a fever of 104 degrees, so I rushed from Tokyo to be at his side. The physician told him that he must have absolute rest, but my husband said, "Tens of thousands of my friends are waiting for me," and marshaled every ounce of energy to continue his activities in Wakayama, Nara, and Mie prefectures.

I, too, had to use all the energy I possessed to keep up with him. The doctor strongly advised me to accompany my husband from that point on whenever he traveled in Japan. The number of activities held abroad increased dramatically and usually entailed meeting with dignitaries, and so at many of these events, it was appropriate to go as a couple.

My husband's mission in life is to be a pioneer. No matter where he goes, he does his utmost to break new ground.

When a group is composed of men only, the interaction can be a little stiff. When a woman joins the group, somehow the mood becomes a little warmer and friendlier. Naturally, the conversation leads to questions such as, "How is your family?" or statements like, "We have three sons." Often, this will break the ice and bring people closer.

Another Soka Gakkai leader in the women's division remembers Mrs. Ikeda's courageous optimism through the following episode:

"There was a time when advertising vehicles driving around the neighborhood blared a constant barrage of disparaging comments about Mr. Ikeda and the Soka Gakkai. When the loudspeaker trucks hit their peak volume near the Soka Gakkai Headquarters building in the Shinano-machi district, Mrs. Ikeda would join us as we all chanted at the women's center.

"'Let's all chant Nam-myoho-renge-kyo. Let's chant it one thousand times today,' she said as she started counting. 'It will be interesting to see what happens afterwards.'

"It was a time when no one could predict when the dark cloud hovering over us would be swept away or what the future would bring. Nevertheless, Mrs. Ikeda always encouraged us to enjoy ourselves, and she displayed great confidence in any situation."

My husband was the person ultimately responsible for the Soka Gakkai, and he had to shoulder many different responsibilities. Nichiren Buddhism explains that the practitioners of the Lotus Sutra will be slandered and spoken ill of and will be subject to hatred and jealousy, and so my husband and I expected criticism and slander.

Even so, some magazines carried unbelievably slanderous material. I got angry because they published outright untruths with no basis in fact. If false rumors that infringe on personal privacy and the rights of the individual can be called journalism, then the profession will be tarnished and lose its true value. Of course, freedom of speech is important, but that freedom should contribute to people's well-being.

My husband would come home late at night, saying he was exhausted. He seemed worn out from considerable mental stress, but he could not fall asleep right away. Lying awake in bed, he would be thinking about something or other. Our bedroom was on the second floor, and when I would get up early in the morning, he would also wake up. There were also times when he would wake up in the middle of the night and ask me to write something down for him. When he was exhausted, I would make a bed for myself in the hallway next to the bedroom so that I could get up early without disturbing his sleep. When we went abroad, I would sometimes sleep on a chaise lounge so that my husband could rest more peacefully. In the morning, as soon as he woke up, he would begin work at once.

On New Year's Day, 1965, my husband began writing his serialized novel *The Human Revolution*. At the time, the Soka Gakkai's newspaper was published three times a week. Six months later in July, however, it became a daily newspaper. The serial was published every day, including Sunday, so the room next to the bedroom was equipped with a writing desk and manuscript paper so that my husband could start writing first thing in the morning.

I was also ready at any time to take dictation. Even so, when his health failed, he said, "I will feel nauseous if I see another piece of manuscript paper," so I removed the paper from view.

How many hours did you sleep every night?

I slept about four or five hours every night. Recently, I have been able to sleep well, but for a long time, our lives were too busy to get much sleep.

When we went abroad, I would unpack the suitcases when we arrived at our hotel.

First, I made sure my husband was resting. In the meantime, I would start cooking rice. Since there were no kitchen facilities, I would cook in the hotel bathroom, using the portable gas stove we brought. This was my particular talent.

Bread did not agree with my husband at the time, so when we went abroad, we brought along our own rice and other things to accompany the rice that my husband could eat such as *nori* (prepared seaweed), soy sauce, and *mochi* (sweet rice) cakes. Back then, it was difficult to find Japanese food overseas, so I had to make do with what we brought. Given the circumstances, the menu was always the same, so I would rack my brain trying to come up with something different to serve.

In 1974, you and Mr. Ikeda traveled to Hong Kong in January, to North and South America in March and April, to China in May and June, to the Soviet Union in September, and again to China in December. The next year, 1975, you went to the United States in January, China in April, Europe and the Soviet Union in May, and Hawaii in July.

My husband's work became even busier during this time, and we were often up until late at night. Communications from around the world would come in at all hours, without cease. There would be telephone calls, and we would send out messages of encouragement no matter what time of day.

My husband's health was not good. He would have night sweats, and yet he had to keep going day after day even under those difficult circumstances. I, too, was becoming exhausted and worn down. At one point, during the fall of 1975, I became sick with liver problems.

Thanks to the support and encouragement of all our friends, however, I fully recovered. I have a strong constitution and, in those days, could go one or two nights without sleeping. Until then, I had never had a major illness. When my husband was suffering with a fever, I thought I knew what he was going through, but I really had no idea. I truly understood what it was to be in physical pain and distress only after I got sick myself. In that sense, I believe that getting sick was actually a good experience for me.

To tell the truth, 1975 was a very difficult time for my husband. The entire Soka Gakkai organization was facing major ordeals, and so I prayed that I could take on my husband's illness in his place. Then, I really did become sick.

My husband was deeply concerned about this. He said: "You've been very foolish. You should know that if you get sick, you will cause concern for everyone." At the time, I thought that even if I got sick, I'd still be able to function.

My illness marked a major turning point in our family life. From that time onward, our children learned to take care of household tasks on their own, dividing responsibilities among themselves. The entire family switched to a new operational mode.

After that, I gradually took better care of myself. Whereas before, I never included my own welfare in my prayers, I prayed much more seriously for the good health and safety of the entire family, myself included, and all of the Soka Gakkai members.

An interesting thing happened during our first visit to China. In China, meetings always take place at a round table so that everyone can easily participate in the dialogue. Each person at the table must contribute to the discussion. When I attended that kind of meeting with my husband, I had always refrained from speaking. But on one occasion, I was told that I could not get away with being silent. When I said, "I'm just tagging along as the maid," the entire room burst into laughter.

Despite this, I was urged to make a statement, so I shared my thoughts in a straightforward manner. I said:

"In Japan, I had always been told that Communism is something to be feared. For that reason, I had come to perceive China as a scary country. After talking with all of you, however, I have come to see clearly that China is a warm country overflowing with love and humanity."

I am sure that my husband, seated next to me, was nervous about what I would say. But our Chinese hosts said, "You speak your mind honestly," and they seemed to open up and trust us.

The person who kindly attended to and guided us on our trip to Beijing, Xian, Zhengzhou, Nanking, Shanghai, Hangzhou, and Guangzhou was the late Sun Pinghua, the secretary-general of the China-Japan Friendship Association. He had been a foreign student in Japan at the Tokyo Institute of Technology and was very knowledgeable about Japan. During our trip, I asked him what Japanese food he enjoyed. He replied, "*Natto* (fermented soybeans), whole sardines, and a sweet popular with students called 'university potatoes,' deep-fried sweet potatoes drenched in syrup and sprinkled with sesame seeds."

Six months later, when we returned to China, we brought those three items with us as a present for Mr. Sun. I remember him being very happy with the gift. I consider that kind of thing to be part of my work.

In the thirty years since, you have made ten visits to China. Indeed, you have opened the way for a long-lasting friendship with that country. Please tell us, of all the friend-

*ships you have made overseas, who has left the most lasting
impression on you?*

I have to say that former premier Zhou Enlai and his wife,
Deng Yingchao, were most memorable. On the last day
of our second visit to China (December 5, 1974), after
we held an appreciation dinner for our Chinese hosts, we
were driven through Beijing at night. Premier Zhou Enlai
was waiting for us at Hospital 305, where he was under
medical care. Our meeting was scheduled for 9:50 PM.
Out of concern for the premier's condition, I was the only
person to accompany my husband. Since the press could
not be present, I took notes to the best of my ability. The
premier had a dignified presence and did not look at all
like someone who was battling illness.

Deng Yingchao seemed to perceive some similarity
between Premier Zhou and herself, and my husband and
me, and showed genuine concern for both of us. We have
had the opportunity to meet Madame Deng eight times.
Each time we met, our friendship resonated more deeply,
and we were moved as we learned of the hardships she
and her husband had experienced together. She invited
us to her residence in Beijing many times. In her inner
garden, she had fragrant flowering crab apple and lilacs.
Smiling, she told us: "Comrade Enlai and I loved flowers.
He never had the leisure to enjoy them fully, but I planted
a variety of flowers in the hopes that they would give him
a peaceful setting in which to relax."

Deng Yingchao visited Japan in the spring of 1979. On

April 12, my husband and I visited her at the State Guest House to extend our greetings. Our meeting room was the Morning Sun Room, decorated with double-blossoming cherry flowers that we had sent earlier. She told us, "Both of you are like family to me."

She also let us know that she wanted to visit our home and Soka University if time allowed. When we showed her photographs we had brought of the cherry trees planted in her and her husband's honor at Soka University, she was truly pleased. One tree had been named "Zhou Cherry Tree" and the other "Zhou Husband and Wife Cherry Tree."

Before we left, my husband mentioned that he was planning to step down as Soka Gakkai president. Deng Yingchao unequivocally admonished him: "You must not quit! As long as you have the support of the people, you must not quit."

The last time we saw Madame Deng was in 1990 (May 28), when we visited her home. As we bade her goodbye, she said, "As a token of our friendship, please accept these." She handed me an ivory letter opener, which she said was a favorite of Zhou Enlai's, and also her own favorite jade brush holder.

Madame Deng was quite elderly by then and had difficulty walking, but she crossed the threshold of the entryway to see us off, leaning on her secretary for support. We got back out of the car to say goodbye to her once again. She continued waving to us until we disappeared in the distance. Her image is forever etched in my mind.

I recall that Madame Deng once told us: "When we were young, Enlai and I promised each other that we would serve the people. We will continue to keep this promise, even in death."

We visited Russia for the first time in September 1974. Rector Alexei Khokhlov of the University of Moscow and his wife, Dr. Elena, welcomed us. Our trip took place during the height of the Cold War, and we were criticized by people in society and even by some within the Soka Gakkai for going to China and immediately continuing on to the Soviet Union. When people would ask my husband why he was going to a country that denied religious freedom, he answered, "Because there are people there."

I agreed with him completely, and his view was affirmed by the warm reception we received from Rector Khokhlov and his wife. We found them to be wonderful, intelligent people with a warm sense of humanity. Our perception of the Soviet Union changed completely after meeting the Khokhlovs. We were delighted to discover that this country that had been shut so tightly behind the Iron Curtain had people of such fine character.

The rector and his wife and all of the people we met who were associated with them were very warm, and we were happy that we could open up wide avenues for new friendships. The rector and his wife seemed equally pleased at meeting us. Through their encounter with us, they said, "We have made a million friends" [referring to the members of the Soka Gakkai, whom the Ikedas represent].

At our hotel, located close to the Kremlin, each floor

had a person on duty with whom we checked our room key. The person on our floor was a middle-aged woman. Each time we passed her in the hallway, we greeted her warmly. At first, she was at a loss how to respond, but after a while, she returned our smiles cheerfully. When we spoke with her, we learned that she had lost her husband in the war. We once again sensed that, in a wife's grieving heart or a mother's prayer, the profound desire for peace knows no borders.

Rector and Mrs. Khokhlov occasionally visited Japan and created a history of heartfelt exchanges with the Soka Schools and Soka University students. Unfortunately, Rector Khokhlov died suddenly at the young age of fifty-one in a mountain-climbing accident. In May 1981, we visited his family and his gravesite to offer flowers.

My husband has done all he can to be supportive of Elena Khokhlov and her two sons. He even offered to act as a father toward the two children. In a message of hope for the future, he wrote, "The triumphant day will surely come when your sons will carry on the ambitions of the rector and become great scholars." Daisaku has taken care to maintain our relationship with the Khokhlov family. In 1992, Aleksei Khokhlov, the eldest son, and his family came all the way to Mie Prefecture, where we were staying.

We have heard that Aleksei went on to become a professor at the University of Moscow at an unusually young age, and his wife is enjoying teaching there also. My husband was very happy for them and commented, "It is just as I predicted."

Because of these initial contacts, exchanges between the University of Moscow and Soka University have greatly expanded. The successors to the rectorship, Rector Logunov and the current Rector Victor Sadovnichy, have both engaged in dialogues with my husband that were eventually published.

In England, we made another special friendship. Historian Arnold Toynbee and my husband also engaged in a dialogue, and for that purpose, we often visited the London residence of Professor Toynbee. The dialogue extended over more than two years. The Toynbees' home was on the fifth floor of a red brick building, and when we ascended in the old-fashioned elevator, the professor and his wife, Veronica, were waiting with outstretched arms. They welcomed us with joy and hugs. Before the dialogue began, Professor and Mrs. Toynbee kindly gave us a tour of their tidy home from one end to the other. The two made a beautiful and harmonious couple, united in working toward a common goal.

Can you share any recollections of your encounters with leaders of Japanese society?

Let me see. I would have to say that both Daisaku and I have many unforgettable memories of our encounters with former prime minister Eisaku Sato and his wife, Hiroko. One night in early 1966, my husband was invited to the prime minister's private residence in Kamakura, where they had an extended discussion. Then, right after

Mr. Sato received the 1974 Nobel Peace Prize, we were informed that he wanted to show the prize to us, and so, in February 1975, he and his wife came all the way to Shinano-machi to visit. Later, after Mr. Sato passed away, Mrs. Sato and I had the opportunity to get together for a discussion that a magazine planned to publish. I believe that this was at the end of 1981.

In the beginning of Hiroko Sato's book The Secret Records of the Prime Minister's Wife, *there is a chapter about Prime Minister Sato's near assassination. In it, she writes about how the would-be assassin entered the prime minister's residence.*

The first lady's account is painfully vivid. It reveals the extent of the prime minister's efforts to realize the return of Okinawa to Japan from American military administration after World War II.

Hiroko expressed to me, in a motherly way, the attitude with which she supported the prime minister for fifty years. She was an incredible optimist. She was magnanimous, and I very much enjoyed my dialogue with her. I will always remember her cheerfully telling me that, as Scarlett O'Hara in *Gone With the Wind* said of life, "After all, tomorrow is another day."

Hiroko Sato was seventy-three at that time. After we completed our dialogue, I remember that I said to someone there: "I have twenty-five more years until I am her age. I wonder if I can continue to be active for as long as she has." Now that I am her age, I hope all the more to offer encouragement to young people.

5

The Smile Award

THE TITLE of this chapter comes from a comment made by Mr. Ikeda: "If I were to give my wife a certificate of appreciation, it would be in the form of a Smile Award." He said this in an interview with the couple in the 1991 New Year's edition of *Housewife's Companion*.

His wife's smile has a special meaning for Mr. Ikeda and his family. When they were first married, besides advising Mrs. Ikeda on the importance of keeping a household accounts ledger, their mentor, Mr. Toda, gave her this clear instruction: "However badly you may feel, wear a smile on your face when your husband leaves for work in the morning and when he returns in the evening."

Ever since their wedding, according to Mr. Ikeda, his wife has faithfully kept the promise she made to Mr. Toda to maintain a household ledger and to greet and send off her husband with a smile. Whatever difficult situations he may have to face each day, that smile must surely give Mr. Ikeda a sense of serenity and assurance when he leaves and returns home each day.

How many of us could continue smiling, even if instructed to do so by a respected teacher? We may keep it up for a few days. Or there may be some who can always smile when seeing someone off. But for a woman to smile on both seeing her husband off and welcoming him home every single day? That would surely be difficult, wouldn't it?

Mrs. Ikeda has said that, when her children were young, they seemed to have thought, "When Papa comes home, we mustn't try to make Mama pay attention to us." This may reflect her devotion to her husband.

This chapter includes excerpts from interviews with both Mr. and Mrs. Ikeda published in the 1990 and 1991 New Year's issues of *Housewife's Companion*. We can see the depth of the family relationships they have built by looking at the conversations of this well-matched couple.

In Buddhism, the bow and arrow are a metaphor for the relationship between husband and wife, with the man as the arrow and the woman as the bow. In Nichiren's words, "It is the power of the bow that determines the flight of the arrow, the might of the dragon that controls the movement of the clouds, and the strength of the wife that guides the actions of her husband" (WND-I, 656).

Mrs. Ikeda says, "My husband often refers to these metaphors." In modern life, sometimes the man is the bow and the woman is the arrow. For many couples, both may be the arrows that fly out into society. In any case, every couple desires a happy and harmonious married life.

Mrs. Ikeda is reserved by nature. As the wife of the SGI president, she says, "I am a common everyday housewife and am not good at being in the limelight." Throughout this book, however, she frankly and generously shares the wisdom she has gained through experience on how married couples can build a happy life together.

Mrs. Ikeda's circumstances have changed since the beginning of her marriage, when her surroundings were the same as most other people of her generation. Their first apartment had only two small rooms and a very small kitchen with a shared laundry room and toilet. There was neither a washing machine nor a bathtub.

Mrs. Ikeda reflects: "What I can do first and foremost is pray. I pray for my husband's safety and for the great success of his work. This I will do all my life. This will never change.

Perhaps Mrs. Ikeda's single-minded devotion and altruistic intentions set her apart. Their effect is undoubtedly felt most by her husband. She has surely put into practice the four family principles guiding the Ikeda household [see page 75].

When you say, "My husband raised me," what exactly do you mean? What did he teach you?

My husband often says to the youth division members, "Young men should be trained, and young women should be raised." There is a nuance of strictness included in *trained* and a sense of nurturing in the word *raised*. I believe that I was *raised* by my husband in this sense. In the area of faith also, I feel that my husband has taught me everything, including enabling me to be aware of the mission for which I was born into this world. When I have been late doing something or when I have made some mistake in judgment—not in our private life but in relation to our public function—he has been strict.

There was one incident that affected me deeply. My husband had asked me to send a photograph to someone whose younger brother was seriously ill. My husband had taken the picture with him and his family during a visit to encourage the ailing man, and so when the photo was ready, my husband asked me to send it. It took me four or five days to get around to sending it, because I thought I should also write a letter to accompany it. We later found out that the photograph arrived two or three hours after the younger brother died.

My husband strictly admonished me about this. I had no excuse. I was extremely sorry and regretted that I had not sent the photo sooner. I'm fairly certain it was the first time that I was so shaken on account of something I had done. Needless to say, this was a severe lesson for me.

When my husband has admonished me, it has never been without good reason. On that occasion, I voiced my regret that I hadn't sent the photo sooner. In response, he said, "Even if you express regret, there is nothing you can do about it now."

My husband is a born educator. No matter what the situation, he encourages each person to move forward cheerfully and with hope. He does this with me and with the children as well.

In the words of Mr. Ikeda:

"A wise mother is like the sun, making possible the growth and happiness of her children. A wise wife makes her entire household happy. A wife or a mother's smile also extinguishes any discord in the family. Nothing is greater than this. It is more powerful than words. Without a wife's smile, the family cannot become a tranquil oasis."

Please tell us what you alone know about what the president is like.

I think the word *sincerity* exactly describes the real Daisaku Ikeda. He always keeps his promises. He always does his very best to put people at ease, make them happy, and help them enjoy life. Ultimately, his public face and his private face are exactly the same.

As I observe from the sidelines, I am frequently concerned that he is exhausting himself. He is a man of action who is committed to his work, and his mind is always considering eight or ten things at a time, except perhaps when he is sleeping. This is why I try to make him rest. But then, the moment he opens his eyes, his brain starts working again, and his attention goes to many places. It's just the same now as when he was younger. Every day, he will sit at his desk to read a book, write a manuscript, or compose a poem. He never wants to quit working, so I am the only one who can restrain him even a little and urge him to conserve his energy.

My husband says, "I can understand getting angry with someone for not working, but I can't bear it when someone gets angry with a person for working too much." Also, my husband meets many people in the course of his work, and he is very aware of and considerate of their needs. He is kind and caring when talking with someone. He knows how to show appreciation by shining the spotlight on people who are working hard unbeknownst to others.

Since I have been with him for such a long time, I have learned a lot of good things, but still there are many times when I realize something for the first time after my husband points it out to me. Therefore, I often liken my husband to a hare and myself to a tortoise.

Actually, I would rather think of us as a crane and turtle combination [a reference to the symbols for longevity and devotion in marriage]. I hope I can help my husband live a much longer and healthier life.

Daisaku, Hiromasa, and Kaneko, 1954.

Opposite, above: Hiromasa, Daisaku, and Kaneko at an airplane show, 1954.

Opposite, below: The Shuzanso Apartments in Sanno, Omori. The Ikeda family lived here for nearly three years in the room on the first floor on the left.

The Ikeda family home in Kobayashi-cho, Ota Ward, Tokyo, from 1955 to 1966.

Daisaku with Hiromasa on a family outing in the resort area of Hakone, 1955.

(Left to right) Hiromasa, Shirohisa, Takahiro, and Kaneko
in their garden at home in Kobayashi-cho, Ota Ward, Tokyo,
August 1958.

On the day Daisaku Ikeda is inaugurated third president of the
Soka Gakkai, May 3, 1960.

Hiromasa, Shirohisa, and Takahiro at home in Kobayashi-cho, Ota Ward, Tokyo, May 1960, around the time their father becomes Soka Gakkai president.

Kaneko in Kyoto, August 1960. *(Photo credit: Daisaku Ikeda)*

Above: (Left to right) Daisaku, Shirohisa, Takahiro, and Kaneko in the gardens of Mukojima Hyakkaen, Tokyo, March 1961.

Left: Kaneko, March 1964.
(Photo credit: Daisaku Ikeda)

Left:
(Left to right)
Kaneko, Takahiro,
Shirohisa, and
Hiromasa in
Kobayashi-cho,
Ota Ward, Tokyo,
November 1964.

Right:
(Left to right) Takahiro,
Kaneko, Shirohisa,
and Hiromasa at home
in Kobayashi-cho,
Ota Ward, Tokyo,
November 1964.

Left:
(Left to right)
Hiromasa, who is
just starting junior
high; Shirohisa,
sixth grade;
Takahiro, second
grade; and Kaneko,
May 1966.

Below:
Letters and
postcards sent
by Daisaku Ikeda
to his children
when he traveled
overseas.

By the front door of the Ikeda home in Shinano-machi, Tokyo, April 1967. (Back row, left to right) Kaneko; Shirohisa, who is just starting junior high school; Hiromasa, in his second year in junior high school; (front row) Daisaku; and Takahiro, a third-grade student.

Left:
(Left to right)
Daisaku, Kaneko,
Takahiro, and
Hiromasa
surrounded by
ginkgo trees at the
Meiji Shrine Outer
Garden, Tokyo,
October 1967.

(Left to right) Kaneko, Daisaku, Takahiro, Shirohisa, and
Hiromasa in Shinano-machi, Tokyo, March 1969.

A quiet moment in Shinano-machi, Tokyo, March 1969.

(Left to right) Kaneko; Daisaku's mother, Ichi; Daisaku; Kaneko's mother, Shizuko; at Shinano-machi, Tokyo, May 1970.

The fragment of a mirror that
once belonged to Daisaku Ikeda's
mother, Ichi.

At the home of British historian Dr. Arnold Toynbee in London,
May 1972. (Left to right) President Ikeda; Dr. Toynbee; Dr. Eiichi
Yamazaki, SGI Europe leader; Kaneko Ikeda; and Veronica Toynbee.

At home in Shinano-machi, Tokyo, November 1972.

In Shinano-machi, Tokyo, April 1973.

At home in Shinano-machi in preparation for the New Year's
holiday, November 1973.

Kaneko in her kitchen in Shinano-machi, Tokyo.

■

Mr. Ikeda says the following:

"Rather than think only of myself, I try to give everyone hope so that they can live happily and harmoniously together. What lies in store for humanity? What will the future hold? It is with these things in mind that I continue to exert myself.

I have no need for material wealth. I simply want to live a life in which I can impart hope to many people. This is my feeling, and I think my wife feels the same."

■

Your husband says that you have always supported him.

I am neither strong nor wise, but my husband and I pray together and firmly believe in the power of faith and good fortune, something that I am continually learning from him. If one prays earnestly and wholeheartedly, doors will always open.

What I can do first and foremost is pray. I pray for my husband's safety and for the great success of his work. This I will do all my life. This will never change. I, personally, am just an ordinary housewife who would rather not be center stage.

Although Daisaku is in the public eye, I have always wanted to be of service in the background where I can create a family life in which he can relax comfortably and where I can do my best to look after his health. His sphere of activities, however, has expanded to include the entire world, so I accompany him on his overseas trips. Although my preference is to support from behind the scenes, I no longer have the option of remaining in the shadows. My husband isn't young anymore. Since I want him to continue to work with increasing vigor on behalf of everyone, I see my role as guardian and protector becoming even more essential.

Here is how Mr. Ikeda sees it:

"My wife would look over the letters and reports from members, even after I had gone to bed. She was concerned about my health and would pray for me late at night all by herself. Even when times were difficult, she would pray steadfastly and with conviction for victory with absolute justice. My victory is my wife's victory."

Whether in Japan or overseas, I have done my best to create opportunities to meet and talk with members of the women's and young women's divisions who are working so hard and so heroically. Even for people with strong faith, such things as illness, financial troubles, or lack of understanding from those around them can become obstacles and cause them to worry and become disheartened. I feel that it is my role to listen with a sympathetic ear during those times.

The members of the Soka Gakkai women's division are so very busy. They manage their households, care for young children and, in addition to their work, participate in Soka Gakkai activities. It is normal for them to assume three or four roles. Switching back and forth among those roles is challenging. I understand completely, because I have had the same experience. I have listened to many of their stories, and I know how hard they are all working. They have my wholehearted respect.

In 1988, May 3 was designated Soka Gakkai Mother's Day. On that occasion, the members of the Kansai women's division sent Mrs. Ikeda the following poem in appreciation for all she has done:

No matter how turbulent the storm, your smile never fades.
Sometimes a kind nurse, sometimes a caring nutritionist, your
wise mothering of your sons is the way of peace and
happiness.
Your warm, clear voice, your wise and dignified manner,
Your silent encouragement launches us on a voyage of hope,
And our appreciation overflows from the bottom of our
hearts.

By popular demand, the titles of honorary head of the Soka Gakkai women's division and of the Soka Gakkai

International's women's and young women's divisions were conferred on you. What's more, you have received honorary professorships and degrees from six universities around the world—the first from Flores University in Argentina—and have been named an honorary citizen of more than one hundred cities worldwide. This is something of which all the women of Japan can be proud.

I am humbled to have received these accolades when all I have done is accompany my husband on his travels. We joke that I am the garnish that comes with the sashimi.

My honorary citizenships were conferred based on the outstanding examples of national and municipal citizenship set by the women of the Soka Gakkai International who contribute to their societies in the countries where they live. I have humbly received these honors as a representative of these women, in hopes that doing so will encourage the younger generation. My husband congratulates me in a playful manner when I receive an honorary title by clapping with his two index fingers.

Here is a comment on home and family from an interview with Mr. Ikeda:

"The Japanese word for *family* consists of the Chinese characters for *house* and *garden*. The house represents the physical dimension of food, clothing, and shelter. The garden represents the spiritual dimension. These two aspects make up a family.

"With the high price of real estate, most people can't afford much of a physical garden. However, if one's internal garden — that is to say, the heart — is filled with blossoming flowers and the chirping of birds and insects that changes with the seasons, then that contributes to a happy household. The soil from which this garden grows is the expansive feeling of love.

"Of course, extreme poverty is a tragedy. Ultimately, though, happiness is unrelated to whether one has money. What is happiness? What is unhappiness? Happiness cannot be bought in a department store. But anyone with a heart can have a wonderful 'garden of happiness.'"

One's thoughtfulness and personal appearance are important every day. I believe that this extends to cosmetics. Even if a woman stays at home, I think she should get into the habit of attending to her personal appearance the first thing in the morning, including putting on her makeup.

There is a phrase in a Buddhist text that goes, "as a woman refuses to part with her mirror" (WND-1, 1036). Women should never part with their sense of composure. We need to take time to stop and converse with the flowers, listen to beautiful music, and sigh with appreciation at the sight of a beautiful painting.

What is your favorite song these days?

My favorite song is one brought to my attention by someone who wrote to me recently. It's called "Like a Flower
Blooming in the Meadow," and it begins: "Like a flower
blooming in the meadow, I am swayed by the breeze.
Like a flower blooming in the meadow, I refresh whoever
passes by" (lyrics by Masami Sugiyama, melody by Asei
Kobayashi).

In her letter, this person wrote: "I took the liberty of
considering this song 'Mrs. Ikeda's Song.' I have sung it to
myself throughout the years as I have traversed the mountains and valleys of life while overcoming all its difficult
and sad experiences." I was humbled to read this letter
and have been listening to this song ever since.

In the sense of bringing such overlooked things to light,
my husband often focuses his camera lens on things like
flowers blooming in a meadow, as can be seen in his *Ren-
dezvous with Nature* photo books.

*Have you ever received a birthday present from your
husband?*

> *We are married,*
> *and as husband and wife,*
> *we have built happiness*
> *for the three existences of life,*
> *this true and reliable path of ours.*
> (February 27)

I copied this poem into my diary. My husband wrote it for me as a birthday present. On my birthdays, the children have a birthday party for me, and this seems to jog my husband's memory.

On those occasions, when he has time, he will write a haiku or a verse for me. I am not a poet. I only transcribe my husband's poems. My husband calls me his record keeper.

Having recorded these things over time, one would think that I would become a skilled writer. But occasionally, when Daisaku asks me to complete the latter half of a haiku that he has started, he laughs at the way it turns out.

I am very aware that just being in close proximity to my husband does not at all guarantee that I will become a good poet.

With wry humor, Mr. Ikeda shares his view in the following excerpt from an interview:

"When I publish a book, I often write a poem for my wife. I hope that this will make up for the times when I occasionally forget her birthday. Besides that, there is an age when you are supposed to remember a woman's birthday and an age after which you are not supposed to remember.

"I have taken photographs of my wife. I have tried to write poems for her, but, when we are face to face, we laugh or she scolds me, and it seems that we are too close. So, the poems for her never turn out quite right."

~~~~~~

Please share some favorite words of yours for the encouragement of our readers.

Some words of wisdom that I like the best were sent to me by my husband. He wrote, "Complaints erase good fortune. Grateful prayer builds happiness for all eternity." This means that we must have a positive outlook in everything we do. I have made this a personal habit.

My husband also sent me the following poem:

Today, don't give up.
Today, take heart,
Along this path we pledged to follow.

I, along with my husband, have experienced my share of turmoil in life, and this has strengthened me. Somewhere along the way, I found that nothing surprises me anymore.

What kind of message would you like to send to young women today?

I often send these words to young married women: "Become a kind wife, a strong mother, and a capable leader in the Soka Gakkai women's division."

Please tell us what hobbies you have now and what it is that gives you meaning in life.

My greatest reason for living is to give people hope and strive with all my heart to encourage others in all their endeavors. This might go beyond what you would normally think of as a hobby. The joy that I gain from this is enough.

Here Mr. Ikeda has the final word:

"My wife is my life companion, and, at times, my nurse, my secretary, my mother, daughter, or younger sister. But most of all, she is my comrade-in-arms.

"If I were to give my wife a certificate of appreciation, it would have to be in the form of a Smile Award. In many ways, this sums up my feelings.

"Most of all, I want my wife to be healthy and stay vibrant and youthful forever. She is the one who knows, truly knows best, all about me and what is in my heart. And I am the one who knows best her honesty and bravery. My marriage to my wife has brought me the most happiness in life.

"This is why I feel that, when we are reborn in the next life and the life after that and for eternity, I hope we can be together."

Epilogue

HERE IS A LOOK at Mr. and Mrs. Ikeda as a couple, in an excerpt from an article titled "The Hospitality of the Ikeda Family" written for the magazine *Women and Living* (winter issue, 1974) by legendary journalist Takaya Kodama:

> When Mrs. Ikeda says something, Mr. Ikeda play-
> fully taps her shoulder and says, "I don't mind, I
> don't mind." Another comment, another tap. "It's
> OK, it's OK," he says. Tap. "Don't worry, don't
> worry." She does the same to him. "I know, I know."
> And the playful tapping goes on.

In each tap, Mr. Kodama sensed the secret of why such an astoundingly large number of people refer to Mr. Ikeda as "Sensei," or "teacher."

Mr. Kodama writes: "The act of saying 'I know' while tapping [his wife on the shoulder] may express a shyness [typical of Japanese men]. Those who consider themselves cultured or count themselves among the intelligentsia may either envy or look condescendingly upon such honest and unaffected behavior."

Without the trappings of culture or refinement, when a person is stripped down to the most essential core of human existence, an ultimate essence of humanity remains, as it does with Daisaku Ikeda. As his dialogue (1972–73) with Professor Arnold Toynbee illustrates, Mr. Ikeda is a versatile and discerning person clothed in many different layers of accomplishment and eminence.

> Mr. Ikeda's habitual light shoulder tapping, which I observed before, was a superb gesture. Now, when he opens the sliding doors of the Japanese-style room while fastening the cord of his *haori* jacket, and when his wife enters, saying, "It's been a long time since I saw you last," I smell a whiff of incense.
>
> Mr. Ikeda hosts a tea ceremony for me, then stands up, saying, "Oh no, my legs have fallen asleep, and I have to perform my evening prayers."
>
> I ask, "Are you burning incense in the room?"
>
> "No," he answers, surprised.
>
> "Is it potpourri packets?"
>
> "No. I am not the potpourri type."
>
> Still pursuing the scent, I continue, "Does your wife wear perfume?"
>
> He calls out to Mrs. Ikeda: "Are you wearing perfume?"

"No," she answers.

"I know," he says. "It must be the room. We burn incense in here for the morning and evening prayers, and the scent permeates the room."

"That must be it," says Mrs. Ikeda. "We don't notice it because we've grown used to it."

With that, Mr. Ikeda begins to clown around. He taps his wife's shoulder and jokes, "Mrs. Ikeda, please wear perfume sometimes."

Mrs. Ikeda's greeting to Mr. Kodama reveals that she had met him before. That was during his first interview with her four years earlier. Mr. Kodama wrote: "The lady of the house looks the same as I remember her. She still seems as if she just graduated from high school and only recently stopped wearing her school uniform."

After the nearly four-hour interview, Mr. Kodama asked her: "How are you doing? Are you relieved that it's over?" Mrs. Ikeda answered forthrightly: "Yes. It was much harder than any test I ever took in high school."

Mr. Kodama wrote, "Mrs. Ikeda did an excellent job in responding to my questions."

Both Mr. and Mrs. Ikeda share a forthrightness that is not restrained by the opinions of those around them. When the Kodama interview was almost over, Mr. Ikeda reportedly asked in a playful tone, "Are we almost through being tortured by your questions?"

Mr. Kodama responded: "Yes. I suppose these questions must be an ordeal."

Most people would answer: "Oh, no. It's OK. That's your job," even if they felt differently. Incredibly, Mr. Ikeda replied: "Yes. They are an ordeal."

In Mr. Kodama's words, "To hear someone call an interview an ordeal and say it in a way that leaves no trace of unpleasantness was refreshing."

The Ikedas' warm hospitality is further illustrated in the following anecdote:

> The night before my visit to the Ikeda home, our editorial department sent my latest work to Mr. Ikeda. He was extremely busy with work until late that night, and noon the following day was a deadline for him to submit his manuscript to a newspaper. Even so, he and his wife read my work. They didn't just go through the motions of reading. They shared impressions of what I had written that they only could have gained from reading it carefully, perceiving even what was implied between the lines.

What Mr. Kodama referred to as "warm hospitality" was not the refreshments he was served or anything tangible. It was the considerable effort and thought that went into their warm reception of him, a custom that they have lavished on guests since the beginning of their marriage.

Mrs. Ikeda's sister-in-law affirmed this: "They put so much concern and thought into welcoming guests. When Mrs. Ikeda is away, I step in for her. Mr. Ikeda always reminds me to be kind, polite and pleasant, but I know that I am no match for Kaneko Ikeda."

Mr. and Mrs. Ikeda's wedding took place on May 3, 1952, at a temple called Kanki-ryo in Nakano Ward in Tokyo. It was a Buddhist wedding. The date May 3 has special meaning for the Ikeda family. Their revered teacher, Josei Toda, was inaugurated second president of the Soka Gakkai on that day the previous year, and so Toda chose May 3 as the day of the couple's departure. This he did out of consideration for Mr. Ikeda, his closest disciple. Also, it came right after the seven-hundredth anniversary of the establishment of Nichiren Buddhism. Then, on that same day eight years later, in 1960, Mr. Ikeda was inaugurated third president of the organization.

Mr. Ikeda wrote about his wedding in his best-selling book *On Women* in 1974:

> In due time, I got married. We held the wedding on May 3, 1952. We had a ceremony and a reception, but we definitely did not extend ourselves beyond our means. It was an extremely simple affair, but our mentor and close friends helped us celebrate. It was a truly heartwarming occasion.

In another essay, Mr. Ikeda describes the determination that he and Kaneko felt:

> We both shared the same goals and understanding, and we promised each other that we would devote ourselves to the welfare of society and work to benefit people. Our resolve is still the same, even now, and I am sure that it will be the same in the future.

> And so, it is not a choice between sacrificing one-self for society or disregarding society in favor of one's happiness. As we put our resolve into practice, we expected to experience happiness. In our situation, the success or failure of our marriage depended on establishing a new family that would be the nurturing environment supporting our work in society. Thus the magnitude of our wedding celebration was completely irrelevant. (*The Family Revolution*, Kodansha, 1966)

In his book *On Women*, Mr. Ikeda writes, "My marriage is the treasure of my life." He adds:

> The aspect of my life that most concerned my wife was my eating habits. Her main job became restoring me to better health from my weak constitution.
>
> When I married, not only did I get a wife, at the same time I acquired a superb nurse and dietitian. I feel that I have been able to sustain my intense schedule of activities from that time to the present thanks to the efforts and good sense of my wife.

In this way, the couple began their married life in rented rooms in Mita in Tokyo's Meguro Ward, holding in their hearts the truism that "winter always turns to spring."

For Mrs. Ikeda, the Ikeda household was a meeting place and a workplace that entertained a continuous stream of guests. Her amazing energy is confirmed by a story shared by a senior leader in the Soka Gakkai women's division:

> I remember that Mrs. Ikeda once said, "I am with my husband now perhaps because of some good fortune in my past." She continued: "And because of that, I am where I am today. I am so grateful. It is all due to the good fortune from my past."
>
> She also told me: "Good fortune is created by oneself and must be continually accumulated. If not, when it starts to crumble, it falls like rocks tumbling down a hill. This is why I want, as much as I can in my own way, to advance into the future, all the while accumulating good fortune in the present."

In chapter five, Mrs. Ikeda refers to her favorite words of wisdom from her husband, who said: "Complaints erase good fortune. Grateful prayer builds happiness for all eternity." Mrs. Ikeda explained: "This means that we must have a positive outlook in everything we do. I have made this a personal habit."

The good fortune of the Ikeda household is based on the meticulous accumulation of good deeds, one by one. What started out as a small blessing has snowballed into many blessings. Mrs. Ikeda had already learned in childhood the art of turning minuses into pluses and thus learned to create good fortune.

Kaneko Ikeda describes her family situation in these terms:

"My mother had a weak physical constitution, so my older sister and I helped out a lot with the housework. Since I also had a younger brother, I learned perseverance and restraint because the situation required it."

A housekeeper in the Ikeda home reported: "Mrs. Ikeda's mother told me: 'She was such a patient child. Even if she had a fever and was in distress, she never complained.'"

"I was the third of four children, and so I wasn't given much attention in the Shiraki household," Mrs. Ikeda recalls. "But that was a fortunate thing for me, and it helps me even today." Because of that, her family members don't hold her to being in regular contact, something she feels grateful for because it allows her to place a priority on her efforts for the Soka Gakkai."

President Ikeda nicknamed their three sons "The Big Three." The oldest, Hiromasa, was born in 1953 and is an SGI vice president. Josei Toda named him, exclaiming with a satisfied smile: "Isn't it a fine name? He could become a man of letters with a name like that."

Hiromasa recalled an experience with his father, who is fond of cherry blossoms: "We were admiring a flurry of falling petals. I turned to my father and said, 'A blizzard of flowers.' He picked up from there and said, 'On my father's shoulders.' Then my mother added, 'On my mother's hair.'"

"A blizzard of flowers: on my father's shoulders, on my mother's hair" became a memorable verse created by mother, father, and child. This occurred at a time when Hiromasa was considering his future career. He said: "One evening, after our prayers, my mother gave me a word of advice. She suggested,

'You have benefited from your association with the Soka Gakkai organization, so you should devote yourself to it.' Her words helped me make up my mind." With his mother's words in his heart, Hiromasa left for Osaka, where he became a teacher of social studies at the Kansai Soka Schools.

The third son, Takahiro, now a trustee of the Soka Schools as well as a vice president of the Soka Gakkai, was fascinated by astronomy. It seems he was a passionate boy who was something of a problem child. Mr. Ikeda wrote about the back-and-forth tussles among mother, father, and child in an essay, "Thoughts on My Life—My Three Sons and I," published by Shodensha in 1976:

> Speaking of discovery of the self, this occurred to Takahiro, my third son, when he became completely captivated by stargazing in his first year of junior high school. His interest began about three years earlier, when a close family friend gave my second son a telescope. When Takahiro looked through it and saw the rings of Saturn, he became extremely excited. He insisted that he needed a telescope that was suitable for serious stargazing, so we took him to a specialty store.
>
> When we entered the store, Takahiro immediately pointed out the telescope he wanted. It turned out that it was a powerful one, intended for scientific observation. My wife firmly opposed this choice, saying that he would soon grow tired of this sudden passion, so it would be better to buy one that was

more like a toy. The boy wouldn't hear of it and stubbornly clung to his choice, finally sitting down in front of the telescope and refusing to budge. Caught in the crossfire, I tried in vain to persuade both sides to compromise. If the truth be known, I, too, had become captivated by the rings of Saturn. So, I persuaded my wife to approve, and ultimately we bought the telescope. I'll never forget the amused expression on the salesperson's face as he observed our family decision-making dynamics.

Finally won over by his son's passion for astronomy, Mr. Ikeda's reflections on the situation led to further insights: "I felt that having something to be absorbed in is a good thing, especially for young people, who are filled with curiosity. When this happens, they often transcend the framework of classroom education and soar to boundless heights. Adults often try to nip these sprouts of curiosity in the bud based on their own limited preconceptions, and this threatens to warp the development of the child."

The Ikedas' son Shirohisa, the second of the "Big Three," as a member of the Soka University staff, actively devoted himself to the students. He passed away at the young age of twenty-nine.

Mrs. Ikeda's younger brother, Shuji Shiraki, and his wife, Miyoko, describe the day they expressed their condolences to Mrs. Ikeda. The day was October 3, 1984. In Miyoko Shiraki's words:

We went to Tokyo Station from the hospital where Shirohisa had been to meet Mrs. Ikeda, who had returned on short notice from Osaka. We were sad and heartbroken, but when we saw Mrs. Ikeda, it was she who did her best to encourage and comfort us. We spoke briefly at the station. Though I cannot imagine the depth of her grief, she was, as usual, restrained in expression.

She stepped off the train gracefully and surprised us by saying, "Oh, you poor things." I remember being puzzled until I realized that she was referring to our being cold. It had been very hot that day. Shirohisa had even remarked on the heat at the hospital. We were wearing short sleeves, but the evening had cooled dramatically. Even at a time like that, Mrs. Ikeda was concerned about our welfare.

Shuji Shiraki added:

After Shirohisa passed away, Daisaku and Kaneko expressed their firm resolve to look after and take good care of Shirohisa's two children. It is obvious that they always think about their grandchildren and are determined to live a long time so they can look out for them. Kaneko and Shirohisa's widow are as close as a mother and daughter related by blood. Kaneko had often said she would have liked to have had a daughter.

Looking back on my sister's life, the only thing

about her that changed after she married is that she got less sleep. Based on what I know from the time I was old enough to be aware of things, my sister has remained fundamentally the same. She has continued in the same direction without wavering.

One youth division member who was at the meeting in Osaka that day tearfully reported the following anecdote to a friend in Tokyo about the grieving father:

> On that day, Mr. Ikeda sent his wife back to Tokyo early, and he stayed until the very end of the meeting. Right up until the moment he had to leave, he was encouraging and inspiring the youth division members to develop themselves. The next morning at the airport, as he was leaving for Tokyo, he told the handful of people who were there to see him off, "I'm entrusting the future of Kansai to all of you."

After the plane took off, the members at the airport cried a deluge of tears, moved by Mr. Ikeda's heartfelt effort and concern toward them, though they knew he was grieving the sudden loss of his son.

The two grandchildren graduated from their father's alma mater, Soka University. Following in their father's footsteps, they are devoting themselves, as their father did, to the path of education.

Mr. Ikeda wrote the following about his wife in his work, *My Résumé*.

I wrote an article titled "For My Children" in the New Year's issue of a women's magazine: "When they fall in love and get married, there is only one thing I will tell them. I will say: 'Don't mind me. Just take good care of your mother.' She regards May 3 as the day of our family's funeral, but ever since that day she has devoted herself to our work, always with a smile. For this I will be eternally grateful."

How does Mrs. Ikeda view her husband, who wrote of her in such glowing terms? A leader in the Soka Gakkai women's division says:

> Mrs. Ikeda always tells us humbly: "The relationship between my husband and me is like that of the sun and the moon. He is the sun, and I am the moon shining in his light. If the sun disappears, I will no longer be radiant."

The same leader adds: "She often says: 'Remember, you don't have to win, just be sure you don't lose. No matter what the situation, live life without ever being defeated.'"

"Live life without ever being defeated." These words illustrate Kaneko Ikeda's experience and determination to honor the life she has lived with her husband and to never turn back.

Here is one of the many poems Mr. Ikeda has written that resonate with his wife's determination:

Forever and ever
May we gaze together
Upon Mount Fuji.

October 12, 2002
In Hachioji
Daisaku

Postscript

A n interview with Mrs. Ikeda and her two sons, Hiro-masa and Takahiro, was carried in the New Year's issue of *Housewife's Companion* in January 2006, a year after the publication of the Japanese edition of this book. With permission, the interview is presented here.

How does the Ikeda household celebrate the New Year's holiday?

Mrs. Ikeda: I am sure that New Year's in the Ikeda family is slightly different from other families. We usually begin our observance well before the ringing of the Joya no Kane [traditional tolling of temple bells throughout Japan] on New Year's Eve. Around nine or ten in the evening, the entire family chants together. This is how we spend New Year's Eve. Then we have *otoso*, the New Year's sake. My husband is served first, then we all drink a cup and have some *konbu* [kelp seaweed], the only thing we prepare. This has been our family's custom every year since Hiromasa was in high school.

Takahiro, who now lives in Osaka, and his wife come to visit on the evening of December 31. Hiromasa used to do that when he lived in Osaka. The entire family gathers.

When the boys were college students, they would depart after our family get-together, and so my husband and I would be by ourselves on New Year's Day. When our mentor, Josei Toda, was alive, we would visit him to pay our respects and wish him a happy New Year. Afterwards, we would attend the New Year's Day activities at the Soka Gakkai Headquarters.

Since we were always so busy, our New Year's Day meals consisted of curried rice and the customary New Year cuisine called *osechi ryori*. Even after our lives settled down a bit, this routine seemed to suit us, so we continue to have curried rice and *osechi ryori* on New Year's.

What are your thoughts on how to enhance a child's personality and individuality?

Mrs. Ikeda: Our children have an abundance of individuality. After we moved to Shinano-machi, each of the boys had his own bookcase. Looking at the books in these cases, you could understand the individual interests and orientation of each boy.

Our oldest son's bookcase contained books on history and related genres such as *The Complete Collection of World Literature* and *The Tale of the Heike*. Our third son became fascinated with astronomy in elementary school, and so his bookshelf was filled with astronomy books. They were books that anyone but an expert would have quite a problem understanding.

You told us how Takahiro was so intrigued with astronomy that he became obsessed with acquiring a professional-grade telescope. When he was a teacher at the Soka Schools, it seems that he put his childhood passion to good use by teaching astronomy to his students.

Mrs. Ikeda: Takahiro started stargazing in the fourth grade. His summer homework was to write a composition about something that interested him. It all began when he was thinking about a topic. A telescope that someone had given us was folded up in a corner of the room, and so his tutor, a college student, put it together. Takahiro waited for nightfall and was able to see the planet Saturn and its rings.

After that, he became completely absorbed. He even stayed overnight in a little shack at the construction site of the future Soka University [in Hachioji, Tokyo] so that he could observe the stars, claiming it was necessary to complete his homework. This was when the campus was being developed, and the construction site was like a mountain wilderness. He used his telescope to take pictures and developed them on site. It amazed me that he had learned how to develop his own photographs. Apparently, his older brother, Shirohisa, taught him how. Shirohisa was a science enthusiast and liked machines. He even built his own cameras.

Though Takahiro immersed himself enthusiastically in astronomy during his elementary school years, his school grades didn't reflect all this effort. I wistfully thought that, if he were going to become engrossed in a subject, it would have been nice if he had chosen a topic that helped his grades. It seems, however, that his interest was later put to good use at the Soka Schools. He was instrumental in initiating EarthKam, a NASA (National Aeronautics and Space Administration, USA) program, the only one of its kind in Japan, at the Soka Schools.

The NASA program was being considered for the Soka Schools, but the schools couldn't raise the money, so the program was at a standstill. Takahiro went into his own pocket to fund the computer system for the program. After that, my husband also contributed something because, he said, it was an important project. When Takahiro was in elementary school, we did not see much of a future in his passion for astronomy, but now we see that his efforts have borne fruit.

It appears that Hiromasa takes after his father with his literary talent.

Hiromasa loves to read. He is always reading something. Now he occasionally writes a column for the *Koko Shimpo*, the Soka Gakkai's newspaper for high school students. A number of his articles were compiled into a book titled *My Path of Youth*, published by Otorishoin Publishers, and already a Chinese-language edition has come out. [The English-language edition is being published by World Tribune Press.]

He is always talking about complex subjects, and when the family is together, my husband often remarks, "If Shirohisa were here, the discussion would probably become even more difficult to follow." Our second son, Shirohisa, who passed away, was the scientific one. Sometimes, before my husband goes to bed, we will all get into a discussion about societal problems. On those occasions, the two boys pose such a striking contrast that my husband describes Hiromasa as "NHK" (the national public broadcasting service) and Takahiro as "Minpo" (commercial television). They are men, so there are aspects of their nature that are inscrutable to me as a woman. Yet, it is still so enjoyable to me when a new dimension of their personalities is revealed, even at their current age.

Strong family ties depend on the mother, don't you think?

I often had to be away from home, and I would worry about how the children were doing. I might have asked about every single detail if they were girls, but, being boys, they disliked probing questions about their activities. So I did not ask how things had gone while I was away.

When I could not attend PTA meetings, my mother would go in my place. People were so used to seeing her that, when I did attend, I would be asked, "What happened to Grandma?" It became standard practice at our house for Grandma and Grandpa to stay when I had to be away from home. The boys may have been a little more restrained with them there, but I felt that it was good for them to have someone at home to look after things.

I often encourage the women's division members to "create a strong foundation for your family." Ultimately, an important part of this is the mother's strength. In reality, a mother cannot look after everything, but I believe that the desire to do so is important.

I also think that the mother of the family should respect her husband and, in the natural course of everyday life, impart to the children that their father is the central figure in the family. This is true even if you know that you are actually the center of the family. I believe it is important for a woman to use wisdom in this area and persevere. Nichiren describes the wisdom of women, saying, "Women support others and thereby cause others to support them" (WND-1, 501). If the family is solid and secure, then children can grow up happy and without worries.

Hiromasa: To achieve this goal, I think it's important to consider each family member's role in the household.

Mothers and fathers have their roles and responsibilities in maintaining the family. The proportion of work that each puts in may vary, depending on the household. In some households, the couple may share the responsibility fifty-fifty. In others, the mother may shoulder 80 percent while the father may take 20 percent. The question is this: To make the family the bedrock of the children's lives, how can everyone help and support one another?

If the family provides a firm foundation for their lives, children have the freedom to devote themselves to their studies and excel. Just as rich, fertile soil will produce healthy seedlings, the family becomes solid ground for the development of fine, well-rounded human beings.

Mrs. Ikeda: This reminds me of when we traveled to the United States in the fall about twenty years ago. In my discussions with members of the women's division there, I realized that divorce was common. Now the divorce rate in Japan has increased, but at that time it wasn't as high.

When I see how divorce can leave children feeling insecure and emotionally devastated, I feel sad about the heavy burden divorce lays on children's innocent shoulders. Although parents choose divorce to suit their own needs, the children often feel that it is their own fault.

I would say that divorce is one of many developments that lead to a vicious circle of social ills. I believe that all members of the family must make an effort to keep children grounded in a solid family environment.

Hiromasa: In our home, our mother maintained her characteristic magnanimity and good humor no matter what the circumstance. When some of the weekly magazines would raise a fuss about the Soka Gakkai or our father, she never let it affect the atmosphere of our home life. When I was a child, my father was falsely accused of election fraud and arrested. Of course, he was later found innocent in a court of law. To my mother's credit, however, I have no recollection of this episode from my childhood days.

This must surely reflect the profound trust that you share with your husband.

Mrs. Ikeda: I trust my husband completely. Because our relationship is so strong, I trust him no matter what happens. When he was arrested on suspicion of election fraud, I recall being absolutely certain of his innocence. I knew that there had to be some ulterior motive behind his arrest, and that in time the truth would surely come to light.

Takahiro: I think that as children we understood that our father and mother trusted each other and were devoting themselves completely to helping other people and contributing to society.

My work as a teacher has made me aware of certain things. In many families, both parents work and are busy

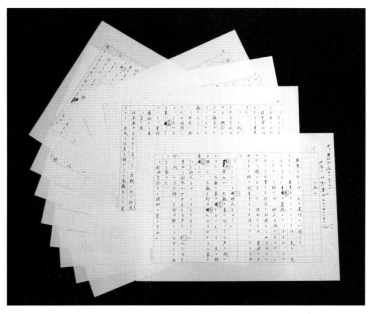

The transcription of part of Daisaku Ikeda's novel, *The Human Revolution*. A note reads, "Because I am physically a little tired, I had my wife transcribe what I said." About 1974.

In San Francisco,
March 1974.

During her first visit to China, Kaneko and Daisaku tour the
Ming Tombs Dam near Beijing, June 1974.

At Tiananmen Square in Beijing, June 1974.

Meeting with Chinese Premier Zhou Enlai at the 305 Hospital in Beijing, December 1974.

President Ikeda hoists his mother, Ichi, age 79, on his back during a visit to Fujinomiya, Japan, April 1975.

(Front, left to right) Rector Alexei Khokhlov of the University of Moscow, President Daisaku Ikeda, Madam Elena, and Kaneko in Moscow, May 1975.

A family moment in Shinano-machi, Tokyo, July 1976.
(Photo credit: Daisaku Ikeda)

Notebooks in which Kaneko kept her diary.

Visiting Deng Yingchao, widow of China's Premier Zhou Enlai, at her home in Beijing, April 1980.

(Left to right) Takahiro, Shirohisa, Hiromasa, Daisaku, and Kaneko in Yokohama, Kanagawa, December 1982.

With the family of the late Shirohisa Ikeda, January 1988.

Kaneko's schedule for February 1987, when she and President Ikeda visited the United States and the Dominican Republic.

In Fujinomiya, Shizuoka, September 1988.
(Photo credit: Daisaku Ikeda)

Kaneko and her mother, Shizuko, age 84, at home in
Shinano-machi, Tokyo, October 1988.
(Photo credit: Daisaku Ikeda)

In London, May 1989.

Kaneko and Daisaku Ikeda in Nagano, August 1989.

In Shinano-machi, Tokyo, October 1989.
(*Photo credit: Daisaku Ikeda*)

Kaneko shares a humorous moment with her husband during a reception for a Chinese delegation in Setagaya, Tokyo, September 1992.

In Mie Prefecture with Aleksei Khokhlov, the son of the late Rector Alexei Khokhlov, and his family, December 1992.

In Hong Kong, November 1995. *(Photo credit: Daisaku Ikeda)*

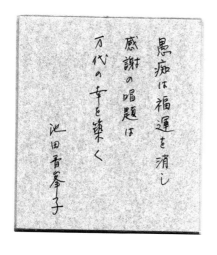

愚痴は福運を消し
感謝の唱題は
万代の幸を築く

池田香峯子

Above: Kaneko's words
to a friend in Bunkyo,
Tokyo, November 1982:
"Complaints erase good
fortune. Grateful prayer
builds happiness for all
eternity. Kaneko Ikeda."

Right: Kaneko Ikeda's
words to a young woman
who was about to marry:
"I am confident that you
will become a warm-hearted
wife, a strong mother,
and a capable women's
division leader."

優しい奥様に、強いお母様に そして
力ある婦人部のリーダーになられますことを
期待しております。

all the time. If the parents simply apologize, saying, for instance, that they are "sorry for being so busy," the children may think that the parents' dedication to their work is something to be unhappy about. I think it is better to explain to the children, "We are doing our best for the well-being of society." To say something like, "I can't spend time with you during the holidays, but please be patient," or "Take care of things while we're gone, OK?" will help children feel that they are trusted.

After reading this book about your mother, what thoughts do you have as her children?

Takahiro: I was born in 1958, so by the time I remember being aware of things, my father was already the president of the Soka Gakkai. When I read my mother's book, I learned much about how things were when I was still small.

When I was little, there were always lots of people coming and going at our house. I remember my father taking me along when he would go to meetings and events. I didn't really understand what it meant for my father to be president of the organization, but I remember seeing him in this role and observing him interacting with members.

My mother rarely could attend my elementary school events and PTA meetings, so most of the time my grandmother attended in her place. A friend once remarked, "Your mother is pretty old, isn't she?"

My father was frequently away on overseas trips or attending meetings in other parts of Japan, and when he came back, he would bring presents and souvenirs from the places he had gone. In those days, gifts or postcards from overseas were unusual, so we were really impressed. When my father was too busy, sometimes, unbeknownst to us, my mother would quietly buy a present on her own and have it ready for us at the appropriate time.

Our mother would always inform us of our father's schedule and the events or meetings he was attending each day. Also, our Soka Gakkai newspaper, *Seikyo Shimbun*, reported on what he was doing, and my mother would point out these articles. We were always informed of his activities. Even though our father was not in our midst, we felt his presence.

As a teacher, I am always thinking about ways to instill in children good values and practices. I strongly believe in providing an upbringing in which values are acquired unconsciously, so that the child becomes aware of them upon looking back at his or her experiences. This was the wisdom of my mother's style of raising children as opposed to, for example, imposing values on children to make them behave in certain ways.

Hiromasa: When my father was appointed president of the Soka Gakkai, I was in my first year of elementary school. I remember that my grandmother took me to the inauguration ceremony, but I had no idea what it all meant.

During elementary school, my mother occasionally

came to PTA meetings, but when I entered junior high school, it was mostly my grandmother who attended. I don't recall that my father came to my entrance or graduation ceremonies.

The fact that our father was always away may seem strange. In an elementary school composition assignment, I wrote, "My father hardly ever comes home." This worried my homeroom teacher so much that she visited our home. It may have seemed strange to others, but it was perfectly natural to us.

Our mother helped us understand and appreciate our father. In her way, she created an atmosphere in which we did not feel that it was a problem for our father to be away. We never felt uncomfortable about it. Now that I think back on it, I realize that our mother made sure that we came to know our father as an important and intimate part of our family.

What was your experience with your father?

Hiromasa: Father used to always tell us, "You must not be a bother to others," and "Never tell a lie." He never scolded us severely when we were young, but he did inspire in us a certain sense of consequence, so that we felt that if we did anything wrong, we would get scolded.

Mother was the one who would be particular about the little things. Father never did that. We implicitly understood from him that we should have the self-respect to not be a bother to others and conscientiously do what we were meant to do.

As is mentioned in this book, when we lived in Kobayashi-cho, our father was away most of the time. After we moved closer to the Soka Gakkai Headquarters in Shinano-machi, he came home regularly and, for a while, it felt a little strange. When he came home, Mother would call us and we would all gather at the door to greet him.

Takahiro: Our father was very kind to us. He feels the same way toward all children. He wants to do everything he can for the students of the Soka Schools and Soka University. Whenever small children are present, he calls out to them and always lavishes his attention on them.

When our father was home, we felt that we must not take advantage of our mother's time or pester her for attention. We knew that we must not expect her to dote on us then. This was a priority that we understood in our hearts. We knew that when our father returned home, our mother would devote herself to looking after him. There were times when he would come home with a fever and go to bed immediately, and she would tend to him.

Hiromasa: We knew that our father was working strenuously in the outside world, so we wanted him to rest when he was home.

Takahiro: Though we were children, we had a sense of why our father was working so hard, and perhaps it was this that made us feel that he was a really great man.

Your father took many photographs of you children, didn't he?

Hiromasa: Thanks to this book, we learned how many of them there are. Now that I think of it, our contact with our father was limited to the time he had between events and meetings. Perhaps that is why he took pictures and gave us presents, taking advantage of the short time we had together. I feel that those photographs represent the brief family time we did share.

At seventy-seven (at the time of this interview in 2005), our father is now very healthy. Back then, I don't think that he expected to live this long. He was in poor health and lived each day as if it were his last. That is probably why he took so many family pictures. He wanted to leave them for the family to remember him by. I marvel at how many pictures we have from our childhood.

Creating a Life of Indestructible Happiness

JANUARY 1, 2005

M Y DEAR WOMEN of the SGI-USA: First, I want to express my sincerest respect and appreciation for the precious efforts you exert for *kosen-rufu* day by day and month after month on the wonderful stage of your mission in the vast land of America.

Unexpectedly, I received from SGI-USA Women's Leader Linda Johnson—whom I deeply revere and love—a request for a message to the January 2005 issue of *Living Buddhism* magazine, a special issue for women. I was deeply humbled but happily accepted her request in the hope that what little I have to share will provide you with some encouragement.

It is a joy that not a single day passes here in Japan without us receiving wonderfully vibrant reports from fellow members of the SGI-USA. My husband is heartily delighted at your splendid activities, saying: "America is the pivotal point, the center, of worldwide *kosen-rufu*. Therefore, nothing gives me more hope than the advancement of our friends in America."

You lend remarkable protection and support, at times overtly and at other times behind the scenes, to the newly born Soka University of America, for which my husband, as founder, and I press our palms together in deepest and sincerest gratitude.

In every country, in every land, women are the driving force of *kosen-rufu*. You, the women of the SGI-USA, above all, are foremost in shining the sunlight of hope and humanism at the grassroots of our organization, while expressing your capabilities in your respective communities and in society as a whole.

I know how busy you are. Many of you work in society as well as take care of your homes. Many of you are raising children. In addition, you take responsibility for many SGI activities. You may have three or even four roles to play in the course of your daily lives. I bow to you in admiration for your untiring day-to-day efforts.

I myself have experienced the difficulty of mentally changing gears to cope with the many aspects of my daily challenges.

It is easy to talk about fulfilling responsibilities at work and in activities at the same time, but putting it into practice is extremely difficult. There is no doubt, however, that all your earnest prayers and painstaking efforts to fulfill your responsibilities at work and in the SGI will cause your life-condition to expand, your good fortune to accumulate, and your life force to strengthen. You will definitely see all your prayers and efforts dignify your existence.

Nichiren Daishonin writes, "*Myo* means to be fully endowed, which in turn has the meaning of 'perfect and full'" (WND-1, 146). It is said that *myo* is the "invigorating" teaching, which means that absolutely nothing is wasted in the world of the

Mystic Law of Nam-myoho-renge-kyo, that everything takes on meaning there. I deeply feel this is true.

"Complaints erase good fortune. Grateful prayer builds happiness for all eternity." My husband once shared these words with me, and I have deeply engraved them in my heart as a guideline for my life.

I am firmly convinced, based upon my own experience, that we can definitely break through our challenges and open up a path to happiness with earnest, wholehearted prayer, based on the power of faith we have learned in the SGI.

I was so fortunate to be one of those who met with and received training directly from the Soka Gakkai's first and second presidents, Tsunesaburo Makiguchi and Josei Toda. My whole family joined the Soka Gakkai in the summer of 1941 because of my mother's illness. She overcame her sickness thanks to the benefit of faith and began to participate in activities vigorously and in high spirits. The abominable war in the Pacific broke out in December of the same year.

I recall that three policemen came to our home to observe from the hallway a discussion meeting being held with President Makiguchi. In the middle of President Makiguchi's talk, they angrily shouted to him time and again: "That's enough! Stop it!" President Makiguchi nevertheless remained as unshaken and resolute as ever.

As I watched how he behaved under such circumstances, I felt: "President Makiguchi is right. The Soka Gakkai is correct." I will never forget that scene. In that moment, I etched the justice of Soka in my young heart.

In the meantime, under the oppression of Japan's military

government, Presidents Makiguchi and Toda were unjustly imprisoned as thought criminals. Some Soka Gakkai leaders, forgetting their debts of appreciation to them, came to our home in an attempt to coerce us into abandoning our faith. Upset by their cowardly betrayal, my father and mother, who were usually very warm and calm, severely scolded them and told them to leave.

Nichiren Daishonin writes, "Although I and my disciples may encounter various difficulties, if we do not harbor doubts in our hearts, we will as a matter of course attain Buddhahood" (WND-1, 283). Also, "This is what I have taught my disciples morning and evening, and yet they begin to harbor doubts and abandon their faith" (WND-1, 283).

Holding on to these passages, which Presidents Makiguchi and Toda taught us, my family strove on.

Those who dedicate their lives to *kosen-rufu* through the SGI, an organization born out of the Buddha's will and mandate, will see as time passes that they are living the most victorious and glorious existences in which all desires are fulfilled. On the contrary, those who leave their friends in the SGI, the "safety zone of happiness," cannot escape becoming extremely miserable in the final chapters of their lives. I have witnessed with my own eyes the strictness of cause and effect expounded in Buddhism.

Recently, my husband wholeheartedly emphasized to the SGI young women: "You cannot capture happiness no matter how much you may chase after it. Happiness is something that follows you. Happiness definitely follows the person who embraces the Mystic Law, the person who has accumulated good fortune. This is the law of life."

I feel exactly the same way. No matter who you are, life

is a battle against problems and worries. Nam-myoho-renge-kyo is the power that enables us to surmount any mishaps and hardships. It is capable of breaking through even the fundamental sufferings of birth, aging, sickness, and death. No one is stronger or more worthy of respect than those who live their lives believing in Nichiren Daishonin's ultimate philosophy while fulfilling the mission of widely sharing it with others.

President Toda would often encourage women by saying, "A women's true happiness and victory start unfolding in her forties." Isn't it true that if we should be too blessed and everything went smoothly from the beginning, we could not experience true joy or happiness in the long drama of our lives? It is precisely because we have to muster courage and challenge our hardships that our lives become youthful and fulfilled.

Regardless of how things may progress throughout your lives, you can win against every obstacle. You will open up a truly fulfilled and eternally indestructible life-condition of happiness at the most crucial, final stages of life, as long as you maintain correct faith, faith for attaining Buddhahood in this lifetime.

A woman's victory in life, which flows into the lives of her entire family, relatives, and descendants like the power of the sun, can impart benefit and good fortune to every person with whom she has developed a bond in this lifetime.

I have renewed my determination to take action for another round of victories together with all the SGI women in the 190 SGI countries and territories throughout the world, including the United States, toward 2010, the eightieth anniversary of the Soka Gakkai's founding.

Rosa Parks, the mother of human rights, who kindly visited

Soka University of America and Soka University in Japan, called out to us to establish in the twenty-first century a world where all human beings lend a hand to one another and offer one another encouragement.

No matter what, the twenty-first century must be the century of peace and humanitarianism and the century of respect for the dignity of life. Toward this end, it is increasingly important to create a century of women. You, the women of the SGI-USA, will proudly spearhead this lofty endeavor.

The Daishonin writes: "Although Nichiren and his followers are few, because they are different in body, but united in mind, they will definitely accomplish their great mission of widely propagating the Lotus Sutra. Though evils may be numerous, they cannot prevail over a single great truth" (WND-1, 618).

Where there is harmonious unity, the flowers of benefit will blossom fragrantly and limitlessly. The SGI-USA women, expanding the wonderful solidarity of friendship, happiness, and peace more than anywhere else in the world, are the greatest and foremost hope for the promotion of worldwide *kosen-rufu*.

Let us always remember to smile. Let us advance cheerfully and joyfully as we continue to win together in 2005, the Year of Youth and Development.

I respect you with all my heart. My husband and I will further deepen our prayers for your increasing good health and long lives. We pray that your esteemed family members will be enveloped by boundless and immeasurable happiness.

Awaken to the Wonder of the Mystic Law

JANUARY 1, 2006

HAPPY NEW YEAR to all of you, my beloved fellow members of the SGI-USA women's division! My best wishes to you for a brilliant, hope-filled 2006.

It is wonderful to see you courageously challenging your lives and working together for *kosen-rufu* with such joy, camaraderie, and dedicated commitment, united around SGI-USA Women's Leader Linda Johnson in whom my husband and I place the greatest trust and confidence. Whenever we receive news of your admirable efforts and heroic achievements, our hearts are filled with profound appreciation and veneration for each of you.

Before I go any further, allow me once again to express my sincerest condolences and sympathy to everyone who suffered loss or damage in the devastating hurricanes that struck parts of the United States last year. I continue to chant wholeheartedly for the wellbeing and security of everyone affected and for the quickest possible recovery in the stricken areas. I also thank all those who were involved in the SGI-USA's tireless relief efforts in the wake of these calamities.

Nichiren Daishonin, though facing momentous difficulties while in exile on Sado Island, wrote to his followers, "I am praying that, no matter how troubled the times may become, the Lotus Sutra and the ten demon daughters will protect all of you, praying as earnestly as though to produce fire from damp wood, or to obtain water from parched ground" (WND-1, 444). Making these words our own, my husband and I are always chanting strongly and fervently that all our fellow members throughout the world will be rigorously protected and that their countries will prosper in peace and security.

I remember a few years ago when a group of women's leaders from South America visited Japan. All of them were pioneers of our movement who had dauntlessly made their way through incredible hardships and obstacles to open a path for *kosen-rufu* in their respective countries. Bowing to them in deep respect and expressing his heartfelt praise and gratitude for their selfless contributions, my husband said to them at that time: "Experiencing many hardships is actually a blessing. If everything always goes smoothly, we won't really be motivated to apply ourselves all out to our Buddhist practice nor, as a result, accumulate great benefit. The most trying times actually present the greatest opportunities for challenging ourselves. It is at such times that we accumulate vast everlasting good fortune that will endure throughout all future existences. This is the realm of the Mystic Law—the law of cause and effect."

I, too, have been steadfastly practicing Nichiren Buddhism since I was a young girl, when I was fortunate to personally meet and receive encouragement from Tsunesaburo Makiguchi, the Soka Gakkai's first president. One thing I have learned from my many years of Buddhist practice is that as long as we base ourselves on the Mystic Law and continue to advance with the Soka Gakkai—the organization dedicated to fulfilling the Buddha's will and decree—everything that happens in our lives has profound meaning. Even if at the time we cannot understand what it is, the meaning will definitely become clear to us later. Above all, because we embrace faith in the Gohonzon, we have the power to transform any adverse situation into something positive, in effect "changing poison into medicine." I strongly believe this with all my heart.

In my youth, I also received training as a disciple of Josei Toda, the second Soka Gakkai president, and devoted myself totally to working for *kosen-rufu* day after day, year in, year out. In the process, I forged the spirit to never be defeated by anything. This is my greatest fortune, and I am eternally grateful for it.

Nichiren Daishonin teaches, "The three obstacles and four devils will invariably appear, and the wise will rejoice while the foolish will retreat" (WND-1, 637). Life is filled with unexpected difficulties and obstacles. They often manifest as different forms of karma in our lives—as conflicts in our relationships with our parents, partners or children, or as problems in the areas of health or personal finances, to name just a few. But when we employ the strategy of the Lotus Sutra—chanting Nam-myoho-renge-kyo—there is absolutely no suffering that we cannot overcome.

A wondrous thing about faith in the Mystic Law is that it lessens our karmic retribution, making it possible to surmount every adversity we encounter. Moreover, it is through our struggles to win in our lives based on faith that we can expand and elevate our inner state of life. This, I believe, is the key to our human revolution and our attainment of Buddhahood in this lifetime.

Nichiren writes, "If the Law that one embraces is supreme, then the person who embraces it must accordingly be foremost among all others" (WND-1, 61). Just as he says, our Soka family is unrivaled in the world; we uphold the world's supreme philosophy of happiness and peace.

Aiming toward our next major milestone in 2010—the Soka Gakkai's eightieth anniversary and the SGI's thirty-fifth—and, still further into the future, with an eye to the ongoing development of worldwide *kosen-rufu* over the next five decades, my husband is now concentrating his energies all the more on training capable people and fostering the youth. He always tries to make time in his busy schedule to meet with as many young people as he can, to form a life-to-life connection with them, to converse with them, and to encourage and inspire them.

Raising successors for the future is also a noble and precious mission that is shared by SGI women's division members around the globe.

In autumn last year, I received a report from Kyushu's Oita Prefecture, where my husband wrote his poem "Youth, Scale the Mountain of *Kosen-rufu* of the Twenty-first Century" in 1981, amid a very turbulent period in our movement. I was, therefore, delighted to learn that now, twenty-five years later, the prefecture young women's leader back at that time has been appointed the prefecture women's leader. I was also happy to learn that the kick-off meeting celebrating the division's fresh departure was attended by all eight former Oita Prefecture women's leaders as well. The prefecture's very first women's leader is now ninety-one years old and continues to be actively involved in Soka Gakkai activities.

Fostering capable people serves to protect the Law, and the creation of a steady stream of capable people gives rise to a mighty river of *kosen-rufu*.

Showing the immense trust he placed in his loyal disciple Shijo Kingo, Nichiren writes, "I have been ceaselessly praying for your sake to the Lotus Sutra, Shakyamuni Buddha, and the god of the sun, for I am convinced that you are a person who can inherit the soul of the Lotus Sutra" (WND-I, 839). The starting point for fostering capable individuals, I believe, lies in valuing and having confidence in each person as a precious heir and successor of the Mystic Law and continuing to pray earnestly for his or her growth.

The Daishonin further writes, "Teaching another something is the same as oiling the wheels of a cart so that they turn even though it is heavy, or as floating a boat on water so that it moves ahead easily" (WND-I, 1086). I have learned through experience that it is important to help all people grow and move forward by believing in their unique missions and potential, patiently watching over their long-term development, and offering them wise words of encouragement and hope along the way.

While I am on the subject of fostering capable people, I thank all of you for your warm support of Soka University of

America, Aliso Viejo, a school devoted to producing global citizens and world leaders.

Early last year, I was fortunate to meet with Kenyan environmental activist Wangari Maathai. With a brilliant smile, she declared that this world, this life, is a wonderful experience and further noted that if we want change, we must be the ones to initiate it. I couldn't agree more. The prayers and actions of one woman can transform her family, the community, society, and even the world. Therefore, what an even more powerful force for change can be realized when women unite in the cause of justice and a refusal to condone iniquity and corruption.

My image of the dedicated women of the SGI-USA, led by Linda Johnson, is that of glorious sunflowers that brighten the hearts of all who behold them. There is, incidentally, a magnificent field of sunflowers near the Soka University campus in Hachioji, Tokyo—lovingly tended by a family that, though not practicing Nichiren Buddhism, is supportive of our movement. My husband took a photograph of their field and sent them a copy. They were touched by his gesture and sent us huge bouquets of sunflowers in return. My husband then presented them with this poem:

> *Spring is here,*
> *Summer is here,*
> *Victorious sunshine is here—*
> *Sunflowers, sovereigns of flowers,*
> *Flowers of happiness*
> *Shining on brilliantly*

Into autumn
Into winter.

A new round of the four seasons is upon us. I hope you will lead the way for SGI women across the globe with the bright, cheery resilience of sunflowers.

It is my dearest wish that you will bring the sun of victory to shine vibrantly in your own lives, as you spread hope and inspiration to all around you. May you also bring beautiful flowers of harmony and happiness to bloom wherever you go through the unity of "many in body, one in mind"—a wonderful solidarity that will serve as a model for the entire world.

My sincerest wish is for your good health and long lives and for the happiness and prosperity of your families and loved ones.

Planting Seeds of Profound Cause

JANUARY 1, 2007

I WISH TO EXPRESS my sincere congratulations on the joyous opening of this Year of Advancement and Victory. We feel elated at the thought that the hope-filled, magnificent sun of *kosen-rufu* will rise anew this year in America, a land we so respect and love, illuminating the entire world with its light.

You are all so very important to me. I am praying with all my heart for your good health and longevity, and that this year you may win a genuine victory in every realm of your life, including your family, work and community, and in your personal goals, as you chant resoundingly throughout the year.

My husband, Daisaku Ikeda, and I make it our practice to start each day facing eastward with our palms pressed together in prayer, sending *daimoku* to the members of the women's and young women's divisions of the SGI-USA and to all our fellow members throughout the entire world.

Due to the time difference, midnight in Japan corresponds to morning in Aliso Viejo, California, when the sun peeks over the hills surrounding the campus of Soka University of America and illuminates the talented young students as they begin their classes and another day of intensive study.

We end each day praying deeply with the thought that we are entrusting the next day of advancement in the global spread of the Mystic Law to our friends in the vast land of America, who have been exerting themselves so dynamically.

Fourteen years have passed since my husband began writing the novel *The New Human Revolution*, into which he has been pouring his whole heart and soul. Including the serialization of his first novel, *The Human Revolution*, he will have completed a total of five thousand installments this year.

There were times in the past when, due to his poor physical condition, he was unable even to lift his pen, and I wrote down what he described to me verbally. Looking back on those days, when he struggled to write with literally his last ounce of energy, I cannot help but feel that his being able to continue to write today, with great composure and in good health at his age, while embraced by the *daimoku* you chant for him, is in itself actual proof of his human revolution through the great power of Buddhism.

The "Triumph" chapter in volume 19 of *The New Human Revolution* begins with his visit to Los Angeles in March 1974.

As you may know, although scheduled to fly from Los Angeles to Brazil, due to the political situation in that country in those days, the Brazilian government would not issue him a visa, and he was forced to cancel his planned visit.

The leaders from Japan who accompanied my husband were at a loss over how to deal with this unexpected turn of events.

But upon learning about the Brazilian government's decision, my husband immediately called the leader of the Brazilian Soka Gakkai organization, offering him wholehearted encouragement over the phone. At the same time, he swiftly began to take action to bring about new advancement for America.

Right away, he decided to visit the city of New Orleans. Our flight arrived in New Orleans late at night on March 14. Our schedule was very tight, as we were to move on to Miami on the afternoon of March 16.

My husband's unchanging credo since his youth has been to live each day wholeheartedly with great purpose, recording in each day a history equivalent to an entire month or an entire year.

While in New Orleans, we paid a visit to the University of New Orleans and met with its chancellor, Dr. Homer L. Hitt, establishing a program of meaningful educational exchange.

Furthermore, my husband attended a number of discussions with students and youth representatives, and held a guidance meeting for three hundred fellow members, thereby sowing deeply many seeds for future development.

A "Happiness Group" was formed of New Orleans and Atlanta members at the time. They have since played a central role, making substantial contributions as excellent citizens in their communities, thus expanding the circle of trust and understanding toward our movement.

As a great result of their continual endeavors, in March 2004, a Friendship Grove was opened in City Park in New Orleans to commemorate the thirtieth anniversary of our visit to the city. The opening ceremony was conducted on March 30, and I understand that Louisiana Governor Kathleen B. Blanco on that occasion declared March 20 World Peace Awakening Day. I also learned that New Orleans Mayor C. Ray Nagin proclaimed this date Friendship Grove Day.

It is our great honor that the Friendship Grove was named after my husband and me (the Daisaku and Kaneko Ikeda Friendship Grove). Indeed, it was my great honor to accept this proclamation on behalf of all the women of the United States and 190 SGI countries and territories of the world.

Nichiren Daishonin writes, "Even one seed, when planted, multiplies" (WND-2, 602). Every action we take for *kosen-rufu*, no matter how unimportant it may seem at the time, without fail becomes a seed of profound cause. As time passes, it grows into a gigantic tree, bringing many flowers of benefit to bloom. I deeply sense the validity of this principle.

In light of the principle of cause and effect, nothing is meaningless in the world of Buddhism. In accord with the principle of changing poison into medicine, there is no impasse that cannot be broken.

Our fellow members in New Orleans faced and overcame the disaster of Hurricane Katrina in 2005, which is regarded as one of the worst natural calamities in the history of America. I understand that SGI members in New Orleans have continued to work hard for recovery, nobly and patiently, hand in hand with their fellow citizens.

We, the Ikeda family, have day and night been sending *daimoku* for the welfare of the citizens of New Orleans.

Nichiren Daishonin asserts, "Though calamities may come, they can be changed into good fortune" (WND-2, 669).

You have all been devoting yourselves to the cause of *kosenrufu*. In light of the writings of Nichiren Daishonin and in the view of the Lotus Sutra, it is an absolute principle that you will enjoy the full protection of all Buddhas and bodhisattvas throughout the three existences and ten directions. The inconspicuous benefit of the Mystic Law is most remarkable and immeasurable. Unimaginable is the scope of the great fortune that the women of Soka in the United States will accumulate in ten, twenty or thirty years through their present painstaking efforts. All the good causes you are making today will turn into a "forest of great fortune," from which will spring a great assembly of highly respectable and able people.

Nichiren Daishonin also wrote, "Only the seven characters of Nam-myoho-renge-kyo are the seed for attaining Buddhahood" (WND-2, 804).

My husband and I have always chanted *daimoku*, wherever in the world we have visited, with the resolve that it permeate the land of that country. We found the time—or more correctly, created the time to do so—even chanting in the car as we moved from one location to another.

In September 1974, in the midst of the Cold War, we visited the Soviet Union for the first time. We recited the sutra and chanted together at the hotel where we stayed while facing in the direction of the Kremlin, praying deeply for the creation of unshakable peace on this planet.

I am truly delighted that Bodhisattvas of the Earth who

uphold the philosophy of the Mystic Law have today emerged in Russia and are working to develop a network of solidarity for the sake of peace.

The other day, I had a chance to talk to a women's division member whose husband's company has transferred him to a politically unstable region of the world, where she will be accompanying him. Speaking to her of my own experience, I encouraged her, "Please chant *daimoku* with a determination to bring peace to that country as early as possible."

Many new people of ability with great promise for the future are emerging today in Japan as well. My husband gave the following encouragement to a new leader of the women's division: "Your responsibility may seem overwhelming, but all the actions you will take for *kosen-rufu* will cause you to become happy and enable your family members, including your ancestors and descendants, to prosper throughout the three existences of past, present and future. For that reason, please work hard."

He also encouraged a young women's division member: "Please live a good life. Please spend your youth well. A happy life lies in living to fulfill your mission. Your happiness exists in living in accord with the eternal principle, or cause, of *kosen-rufu*. Live cheerfully and with conviction, wherever you may go."

He also encouraged a woman facing a serious difficulty: "Do not be sad or pessimistic. Be strong, and overcome your hardship. We chant *daimoku* for this reason."

The Mystic Law is the ultimate strategy for ensuring absolute victory. The Mystic Law is the great principle for securing good health and genuine happiness.

SUA (Soka University of America) has been progressing along a healthy course due to your warm support, having welcomed its sixth class of students.

This school represents the culmination of my husband's undertakings in the area of education. It is a crystallization of the ideas and principles set forth by the Soka Gakkai's three founding presidents—first, Tsunesaburo Makiguchi; second, Josei Toda; and third, Daisaku Ikeda. Availing myself of this opportunity, I, too, would like to express our deepest appreciation to all of you for your dedication in supporting SUA.

Last year, members of the SGI-USA arts division presented an unforgettable performance of heavenly songs and dances, an ultimate expression of "the art of wonderful sound," at the Headquarters Leaders Meeting celebrating my husband's receipt of his two hundredth academic honor.

Because of our friends in the United States, whatever may happen, we can always move forward proudly with hope for *kosen-rufu* throughout the world. I believe that all of you are "sunflowers of hope," who, centering on Women's Leader Linda Johnson, will be the driving force behind every advancement of the SGI in America and around the world.

Sunflowers are native to America and were introduced to Europe in the late sixteenth century. From there, they spread at a remarkable rate, arriving in Japan via Europe in the seventeenth century. Just as sunflowers spread from America to the entire world, gaining popularity among many people, the sun-like smiles, burning conviction and brilliant voices of the women of America will, more than ever before, impart hope and courage to the people of the world.

In November 2006, my husband greeted Ms. Betty Williams, president of World Centers of Compassion for Children International and recipient of the Nobel Peace Prize, together with SGI-USA General Director Danny Nagashima.

My husband asked her, "What has been the greatest support to you in your dauntless activities?"

Betty Williams lost no time in responding: "It is my belief. It is my strong will. It is my courage. We have to persist in any undertaking in which we are engaged. We should not give up no matter what others may say."

Having shared these exact words of Betty Williams with all of you, my respected and cherished friends in America, I would like to conclude my New Year's greetings.

You are noble frontrunners of the Century of Women! This year, again, let us exemplify the greatest unity of "many and body, one in mind" in the world. Let's advance together in harmony, along the brightest, most joyous path in life! Please take care!

Cherishing Each Individual —
Raise Able Successors
JANUARY 1, 2008

MY SINCERE CONGRATULATIONS on welcoming this Year of Capable People and Development, marking a fresh new era in our movement for global *kosen-rufu*. I would like to dedicate this message, with my heartfelt love and respect, to all of the women's and young women's division members of the SGI-USA, as well as to the women of the SGI in 190 countries and territories around the world. I am happy to know that the network of peace and friendship forged among the women of Soka is spreading trust throughout the world.

Sarah Ann Wider, president of the Ralph Waldo Emerson Society, with whom my husband and I have enjoyed memorable encounters, has expressed deep understanding and appreciation for the women of the SGI. The women of Soka, she said, are generous and caring; kind and warmhearted, they brim with amazing vitality. "Just being with the Soka Gakkai women's division members makes me happy," she said. Such beautiful bonds among human beings form the basis of a culture of peace.

Buddhism describes the present age as a time characterized by "conflict and dispute," a period in which people are constantly at odds with one another. In the midst of such an age, it is the realm of the women of Soka—who are striving together in friendship and harmony while encouraging one another—that imparts hope and true joy to many and is becoming an example for women everywhere.

Among the words of Nichiren Daishonin, my husband has frequently shared the following with the leaders of the young women's division: "The blessings and wisdom of the objective and subjective worlds are immeasurable. Nam-myoho-renge-kyo has these two elements of blessings and wisdom" (*The Record of the Orally Transmitted Teachings*, p. 218).

Faith is a source of unfathomable good fortune and wisdom. When just one woman stands up with faith, a pure and refreshing realm of happiness and peace will emerge and expand from wherever she is. When the sun of truth and justice rises, the night of unhappiness and iniquity will be dispelled without fail.

I first met Dr. Margarita Vorobyova-Desyatovskaya in February 1996. A member of the Institute of Oriental Studies of the Russian Academy of Sciences, she is heralded as "the mother of Lotus Sutra research." After losing her husband, she continued to pursue her wonderful research while struggling as a single mother to raise her son. My husband praised most highly her life of devotion to her mission, citing Nichiren's words that one facing difficulty is "as if in winter, but winter always turns to spring" (WND-1, 536).

A woman who has trained and honed herself by weathering

the winter of the severest trials can win for herself a springtime of the most sublime joy. This, I believe, is the true image of hope that results from our efforts to widely spread the Mystic Law.

We were delighted to meet again recently with Dr. Vorobyova-Desyatovskaya, who clearly observed that "as long as the mentor-disciple relationship of Soka endures, the eternal, worldwide spread of the thought and philosophy of the Lotus Sutra is assured."

In conversations with my husband, we have identified three treasures that we value most in our lives. The first is the treasure of having a great mentor, second is the treasure of our comrades in faith around the world, and third is the treasure of able successors.

In particular, when expressing his wishes for the excellent health of all our SGI friends around the globe, my husband has often observed, "When I think of my fellow members who, day after day, are working hard for kosen-rufu amid adverse circumstances, my life fills with even greater power."

Whether nurturing capable individuals or developing our ties of friendship, my husband always exerts himself to cherish each individual.

"When we have compassion, we can bring forth whatever wisdom we need," he has said. And with that spirit, he sincerely continues to do whatever he can to encourage others. Nichiren says, "One is the mother of ten thousand" (WND-1, 131).

If we can earnestly raise a single person to become truly capable—if we can create a sincere and genuine friendship with just one human being—this becomes the first step in spreading happiness to ten thousand people.

Along with all of you who share in the beautiful unity of "many in body, one in mind," I am striving to advance day after day and month after month based upon strong faith. If we pray with renewed determination and initiate fresh action, a new path will definitely open before us, and we will be able to build a new force for peace.

In closing, I share with you a poem my husband has written and presented to the women of Soka:

> *In whatever land*
> *You make your stand,*
> *Brightly will blossom*
> *The joy of life,*
> *Like so many flowers*
> *In their full glory.*

My dear, cherished friends, I am praying from the bottom of my heart that you and your families will enjoy excellent health and great happiness, and for the peace and prosperity of your respective countries.